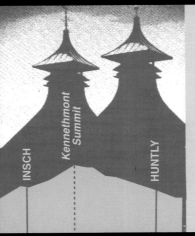

IRON ROAD
to
Whisky Country

MICHAEL PEARSON

A TRAVELLERS & TOURISTS GUIDE TO THE ABERDEEN TO INVERNESS LINE

www.wayzgoose.org.uk
Tel: 01283 713674 / 821472
Copyright: Michael Pearson.
All Rights Reserved.
First Edition 2002 ISBN 0 907864 94 5
Printed in Italy by STIGE Via Pescarito 110 10099 San Mauro Torino

WAYZGOOSE

Iron Road to Whisky Country

Double-track S-curves under the Hill of Christ's Kirk.
Spring sunshine highlights the beauty of the
Aberdeenshire landscape as a four-car train makes
its way between Insch and Huntly.

Heritage & Relevance
ABERDEEN TO INVERNESS

TUCKED away in the north-east corner of Scotland - the definitive, or so it often seems, and which time forgot - there's a railway line which cheerfully defies progress (other than of the most superficial sort) carrying its goodly number of passengers (if sadly little freight) in a way that melds heritage with relevance, an increasingly rare combination. It is not one of Scotland's most celebrated scenic railways. There are no books or videos championing its attractions. Yet on closer acquaintance, it reveals a remarkable depth of charm, and exploring this railway and its hinterland can prove more rewarding than its more obviously picturesque and dramatic neighbours.

WHILST there are no great mountain ranges to stun the visitor, the railway traverses a picturesque sequence of riverine landscapes. East of Keith it adopts the valleys of the Isla, Deveron, Bogie, Urie and Don to facilitate its progress. West of Keith, it cuts more across the grain of the landscape, bridging the Spey, Lossie, Findhorn and Nairn as they make their way to the sea. Its stations serve a necklace of intriguingly historic towns yet to be overpowered by the kind of tourism which can suffocate the highlands proper. Huntly, Keith, Elgin, Forres and Nairn are all unselfconsciously beautiful places of individually self-defining character and atmosphere. Indeed, a week's holiday might cheerfully and rewardingly be spent journeying along the line and spending a night in each, deriving pleasure and amusement from comparing their charms and foibles.

NO little part of this railway route's character derives from its origins. It was the work of two rival railway companies, both of whom desired to forge their own unique link between the Granite City and the Highland Capital. Compromise created a route which outlived every other railway in that corner of Scotland. Today its trains are faster and more frequent than at any time in its hundred and forty year history.

THOSE two railway companies were the Great North of Scotland and the Highland, hugely characterful Scottish concerns, later incorporated into the London & North Eastern and London Midland & Scottish railways respectively during the grouping of 1923. Thus it was only after Nationalisation, in 1948, that the Aberdeen to Inverness line came under

Whisky bonds line the railway on the western outskirts of Keith.

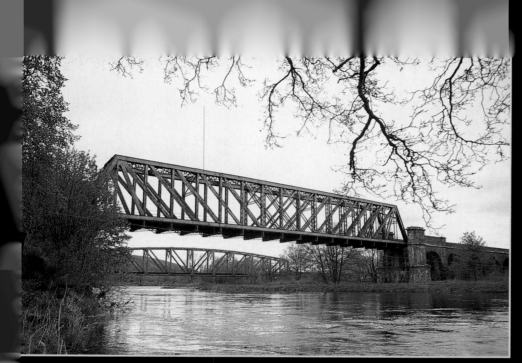

Rail and road bridges over the Spey at Boat o'Brig between Keith and Elgin, both being rebuilds of earlier structures.

THE Great North of Scotland Railway remains much loved. Eighty years after it was rationalised out of existence, a vigorous association of alm three hundred members strives to preserve its memory and interpret it operations and business activities. It was a railway which began badly, g itself into financial difficulties (not entirely of its own making) then pull its corporate socks up and flourished (in its own small and beautiful wa for more than half a century. It was held in much affection by the inhabita of the chunk of Scotland it served. More than that, its very parochiality resulted in a mutual resonance with the topographical nature of the wo it traversed: the landscape defined the railway and the railway knitted together the community. Even today, towns along the line feel a kinship each other which no road link could ever replicate.

A typical GNoS train between the wars (and ownership by the LNER po 1923 did not radically alter matters) would have consisted of an elegar 4-4-0, a turn of the century design by William Pickersgill (described by Hamilton Ellis as 'extraordinarily comely little express engines') painted vivid shade of bright green with dark green edging and lined out in black vermilion, together with a handsome rake of accompanying carriages da red with white upper panels. It does not take much imagination to realis how attractive such an ensemble may have looked, threading its way thro Strathbogie or sauntering under the sunset shadows of Bennachie. Nev realising its ambition of reaching Inverness, at its greatest extent, circa 1914, the Great North of Scotland totalled 335 route miles. You may sh your heid sadly and wonder why only 53 of them remain! Addressing th Great North of Scotland Railway Association at their Annual General Meet John Yellowlees of ScotRail identified the following causes and effects a explanation of the north-east's present dearth of railways: "Beeching's fai to forsee North Sea oil (and) the GNoSR's fondness for building spindly branches to the nearest convenient junction rather than a robust netwo spreading out of Aberdeen".

the control of one organisation, and even then there were ingrained working practises which precluded much advance in the way of timetabling or modernisation. One LNER guard was frequently seen to wring his hands and shake his head as westbound trains reached Elgin, consoling his passengers with the hope that that 'other' company would 'look after them' on their way to Inverness as well as his had! It was left to ScotRail - both in its pre and post Privatisation manifestations - to galvanise the route's resources. Remarkably, this was achieved with little erosion of the railway's inherent atmosphere and character. Eight intermediate stations remain open on the 08 mile route, and it is perhaps not entirely coincidental that only two of them are unstaffed: nothing is so reassuring to the general public as the presence of courteous and informative staff at a railway station.

IN contrast, the Highland Railway has been remarkably fortunate - some 395 out of 492 miles being still in use. Do these statistics illustrate the random nature of railway closures, or is there sound economic reasonin behind the fact that you can still catch a train to Kyle of Lochalsh but n Banff or Fraserburgh? Naturally, these questions are rhetorical. Reams o official reports could be filled with the answers, and still our public transp would be fragmented and irrational, largely because its limitations are obfuscated by mistakes buried in the past; flaws in thinking that our pres transport planning seers would do well to avoid.

IT is at Keith, deep in whisky country, that the two railway companies somewhat diffidently shook hands. Coincidentally, Keith marks the halfway point between Aberdeen and Inverness. Whatever your direction of travel, you would have to be particularly blind to the minutiae of railway engineering and architecture not to be aware of the change in atmosphere and character which remains resonant to this day, so that, in many respects, Keith remains

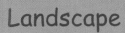

Landscape

Seascape

Escape - by rail!

The imposing signal box at Dyce.

AND what of the future? The Strategic Rail Authority is supporting, subject to 'value for money tests' incremental improvements to the Aberdeen-Inverness route, specifically a new dynamic passing loop in the vicinity of Orton (Map 7) to allow an hourly service to be operated. Creation of such a loop, if accompanied by line-speed improvements, for instance straightening out of the sharp curves at Forres, would enable ScotRail to provide a sub-two hour schedule, maximising stock utilisation and rendering the route even more superior in terms of journey time to the A96 than is already the case. Meanwhile, small improvements, including new and repositioned signalling to allow for modest speed increases, together with refurbishment of the line's signal boxes, have been undertaken by Railtrack Scotland, whilst ScotRail have standardised on Class 158 diesel units for the bulk of the timetable, with comfortable Turbostar units on one or two services. Additionally, the Scottish Executive have provided funding for cost-benefit analysis of the potential for extending services from the south to run beyond Dyce to Inverurie, potentially serving a re-opened station at Kintore. In Britain, public transport takes a constant battering from the media, but in the background, hard-working professionals are ambitious to see our rail network equal - if not overtake - the best that mainland europe has to offer.

ON a personal level, this has been one of the most satisfying lines to research, photograph and present for the rail travelling public's appraisal. Notoriously reactionary, railway enthusiasts might cavil that its rolling stock lacks variety, but that is a general grouse in an era where the traditional locomotive-hauled train, let alone the comfort of compartment carriages, is all but a mellow memory. At a recent Highland Rail Partnership meeting, one delegate raised the concept of a fleet of tourist-friendly diesel units being built on a production line basis for leasing to Train Operating Companies with scenic lines in their service portfolio. It is a radical idea that deserves investigation. The majority of modern units - designed with suburban or interurban operation in mind - are not always ideally suited for such services: they lack luggage and cycle storage space; windows are often not in alignment with airline type seating; the old fascination of a view over the driver's shoulder is no longer available. A new generation of tourist trains could address these drawbacks in a cost effective way. They could include a traditional buffet bar doubling as a tourist information centre retailing locally appropriate souvenirs. It goes without saying that such facilities would prove immensely popular in Scotland. Meanwhile, it would be good to see more use of this undersung route by excursion trains. Perhaps it would also be possible to extend the Aberdeen portion of the Caledonian Sleeper through to Inverness (where, after all, the rolling stock is maintained and serviced anyway) so as to provide important communities like Nairn, Elgin, Keith and Huntly with a direct train to and from London. But let the last words be with R.F.Mackenzie, son of a rural stationmaster on the old GNoS system, and an educationalist by profession though a prophet at heart: "To sit with a cup of coffee or glass of whisky and see the north-east lowlands of Scotland flash past, is this not happiness ?"

MICHAEL PEARSON

Semaphore signals at Keith.

INFORMATION

USING THIS GUIDE

Twelve, north facing, one inch to one mile maps portray the route of the Aberdeen to Inverness rail route and the Keith & Dufftown Railway. Each map is accompanied by a running commentary on matters historical, topographical and related to railway operation. Emphasis is given to the northward journey in each case, but the details are equally relevant for travel in the opposite direction. Towards the rear of the guide a gazetteer gives details of all the stations on the route. This gazetteer gives a brief summary of each place together with itemised information on places to eat and find accommodation, shopping facilities, visitor centres, things to do and useful contacts such as bus links, taxi services and tourist information centres. Where accuracy is essential to the planning of an itinerary you are urged to make contact by telephone to ensure you have up to the minute details.

SCHEDULED SERVICES

Day to day services on the Aberdeen to Inverness route are operated by ScotRail. Currently there are ten trains a day in each direction with an additional working between Aberdeen and Keith and return. One evening working from Inverness terminates at Elgin. At the southern end of the line, many additional trains operate between Aberdeen and Dyce with links to Aberdeen Airport. One afternoon train is extended beyond Inverness to Kyle of Lochalsh, whilst a mid-morning working from Inverness originates in Wick. The average journey time between Aberdeen and Inverness is two and a quarter hours. Services are currently provided by comfortable Class 170 Turbostar and 158 diesel units which provide both first and standard class, non-smoking facilities. Well stocked catering trolley services are available on the majority of services. A limited number of bicycles can be carried on ScotRail services - see opposite.

SLEEPER TRAINS

The Caledonian Sleeper runs nightly (Saturday excepted) between London Euston and Aberdeen or Inverness via Edinburgh (and vice versa) and provides connections to north-east Scotland stations at both points. Very comfortable single and twin berth sleeper cabins are obtainable as well as a certain amount of ordinary seating between London and Inverness. A Lounge Car accompanies each train offering meals, snacks and drinks. **Telephone 08457 550033 .**

CHARTER TRAINS

One or two companies run charter trains and excursions over the Aberdeen-Inverness line from time to time.
Possible operators of excursions include:
SRPS Railtours - Tel: 01698 263814 www.srps.org.uk
The Royal Scotsman - Tel: 0131 555 1344
www.royalscotsman.com
Grampian Railtours - Tel: 01358 789513
Highland Railway Heritage - Tel: 01397 722295

TICKETS & TRAVELPASSES

There are ScotRail booking offices at Aberdeen, Inverurie, Huntly, Keith, Elgin, Forres, Nairn and Inverness. A range of tickets is available from these offices and from the guards on board the trains. For an idea of fares (including current offers, Travelpasses etc) telephone **National Rail Enquiries on 08457 484950** or visit **ScotRail's website at www.scotrail.co.uk**
Tickets in advance are also obtainable from **ScotRail Telesales & Bookings. Tel: 08457 550033.**

BICYCLES

Bicycles are conveyed free of charge on ScotRail service trains. The diesel units which provide most of the timetabled services over the Aberdeen-Inverness line can convey up to six bicycles per two car unit. Reservations are *compulsory* and should be made at principal staffed stations or ScotRail Telesales on 08457 550033 up to eight weeks in advance (12 weeks for the Caledonian Sleeper service) but no later than two hours before the train *commences* its journey.

READING

The Great North of Scotland Railway by H.A.Vallance
ISBN 0 946537 60 7 .
The Highland Railway by H.A.Vallance
ISBN 1 899863 07 9
The Travellers Joy (Story of the Morayshire Railway) by John Ross.
ISBN 0 902343 11 4
Banff, Moray & Nairn's Lost Railways by Gordon Stansfield
ISBN 1 84033 104 6
Rail Freight in Moray by R.I.Smith
ISBN 0 9534534 1 3
Railway Holiday in Scotland by Michael Pearson
ISBN 0 907864 90 2

USEFUL CONTACTS

HIGHLAND RAIL PARTNERSHIP - Lairg Station, Sutherland IV27 4EX Tel: 01549 402896. Email railzzz@btinternet.com
BRITRAIL - rail travel in Britain exclusively for overseas visitors. Very affordable and flexible rail travel options such as the **BritRail** and **Freedom of Scotland** Travel Passes. Visit: www.BritRail.net or call toll-free 1-877-677-1066 in USA and Canada.
ABERDEEN & GRAMPIAN TOURIST BOARD. Tel: 01224 632727. Website: www.holiday.scotland.net.
HIGHLANDS OF SCOTLAND TOURIST BOARD, Strathpeffer, Ross-shire IV14 9HA. Tel: 01997 421160.
Website: www.highlandfreedom.com
GREAT NORTH OF SCOTLAND RAILWAY ASSOCIATION - www.gnsra.org.uk
HIGHLAND RAILWAY SOCIETY - www.hrsoc.org.uk
NATIONAL RAIL ENQURIES - Tel: 08457 484950.
WEATHER CHECK - Tel: 09001 333 111 + 102.

ACKNOWLEDGEMENTS

Wayzgoose extend grateful appreciation to the following individuals and bodies who have helped so much with the production of this guide: Frank Roach and Alison Cavender of the Highland Rail Partnership; John Yellowlees, Dave Prescott and Bill Brown of ScotRail; Barry Hoper and John Macfarlane of Railtrack; John Allison of the Highland Council; Maureen Webster and other members of the Keith & Dufftown Railway; Keith Jones of Aberdeen; Keith Fenwick of Towcester; Geoffrey Evison of Ber; Gil Milne and Jim Morrison of Urquhart; Ron Smith of Banff; Campbell Fraser and David Mcdonald of Forres; Ian Souter of Stirling, Philip Deakin and Andrew Shepherd of the Chillingham Wild Cattle Association; Rupert Brennan-Brown of Porterbrook, and Jimmy Brown of Inverurie.

UNCAPTIONED PHOTOGRAPHS

Front cover: Early morning train through Strathbogie.
Back cover: Dawn over Keith.
Title page: Telegraph poles and Scots Pine near Kennethmont.

The publishers are extremely grateful to the following organisations who have sponsored and encouraged publication of this guide:

Highland Village

Come and discover for yourself the world of Baxters! Every year we welcome over 200,000 people to our Highland Village overlooking the picturesque River Spey. There is plenty of fun for all the family to enjoy and, of course, the famous Baxters highland welcome!

Discover the Secrets of Baxters

Arrive at the Great Hall and find a time for the next Baxters Story and product presentation in our Culinary Theatre. Our chefs will prepare mouth-watering dishes before your eyes and will reveal how Baxters products can be used in imaginative and innovative ways. Tour the19th Century Old Museum Shop of founder George Baxter.

Food & Fun

If you want to sample Baxters produce first hand, why not try one of our two restaurants? Our talented chefs combine traditional Scottish ingredients with overseas specialities and the Baxters passion that makes our food unique. The Gordon Room offers fine modern and traditional lunches together with high teas. The Spey Restaurant provides meals for all the family, together with teas, coffees, cakes and the famous Baxters pancakes!

Speciality Shops

Baxters Food would not be anything without a kitchen and the inspiration of Scotland. Therefore Baxters Highland Village offers four speciality shops for complete Baxters experience. Mrs Baxters Cookshop stocks everything you need for kitchen and table in the atmospheric setting of a Victorian Kitchen. Scotland is renowned for its scenery and to help you enjoy it, the Coat & Swagger shop offers the very best in country wear and accessories to enjoy the mountains, moorland and rivers of the Spey valley in style and comfort. The full Baxters range of products can be purchased in our George Baxters Cellar along with other fine Scottish foods. The Baxters at Home shop provides a unique selection of decorative and practical items for a modern lifestyle.

Arranging Your Visit

If you are travelling some distance we advise you telephone us in advance on 01343 820666. All Coach Parties must be booked in advance.

ScotRail is Scotland's national passenger train operator, providing over 95% of services north of the border. We run four types of service - suburban round Glasgow and Edinburgh; interurban linking the six Scottish cities (Glasgow, Edinburgh, Dundee, Aberdeen, Inverness and Stirling); rural in South-West Scotland and the West and North Highlands; and the Caledonian Sleepers which link Inverness, Aberdeen, Fort William, Glasgow and Edinburgh with London. The Glasgow suburban network supported by Strathclyde Passenger Transport is the largest in Britain outside London. In April 1997 the National Express Group commenced a seven-year franchise for ScotRail during which it has invested £200M in new and refurbished trains, including refurbishment of the Class 158 trains which provide most services between Aberdeen and Inverness. On this route ScotRail have reduced many day return fares, introduced new flexipasses and enabled holders of the Young Persons Railcard to benefit from the 34% discount on all journeys before 10.00. Cycles now go free, and we have supported investment in cycle facilities on trains and at stations. We are the operator of all the stations including Aberdeen and Inverness, and are working with Councils and other stakeholders to improve them -ongoing achievements include better parking at Inverurie and a new lounge and car-park at Inverness.

The Highland Rail Partnership is an association of Highland Council, Perth & Kinross Council, Argyll & Bute Council, ScotRail, Railtrack, EWS, Freightliner, Argyll and the Isles Enterprise, Lochaber Limited, Inverness & Nairn Enterprise, Ross & Cromarty Enterprise, Caithness & Sutherland Enterprise, Moray Badenoch & Strathspey Enterprise and the Friends of the Kyle, Far North and West Highland lines. The Partnership aims to assist the development of passenger, freight and heritage rail business across the Highland area.

Moray Badenoch & Strathspey ENTERPRISE

Moray, Badenoch and Strathspey Enterprise is a local enterprise company which is part of the Highlands & Islands Enterprise (HIE) network. It has substantial powers and resources to achieve economic and social development results across a range of business, skills and community programmes. MBSE has offices in Forres and Aviemore and covers an area from Dalwhinnie to Keith. With a population of 97,000 people in other important conurbations like Grantown on Spey, Elgin, Kinloss, Lossiemouth and Buckie, it is one of the most densely populated areas in the HIE network.

Porterbrook is the UK's leading provider of trains to railway companies like ScotRail. Owned by Abbey National PLC we are making major investments in improving and expanding our train fleets. Porterbrook is committed to working in partnership with ScotRail whose Class 158 trains work most services on the Aberdeen-Inverness line. Our Class 170/4 Turbostars may also occasionally be seen on this route. As part of our commitment to partnership with ScotRail we have worked together and with the Scottish Cycle Challenge Fund to double the cycle-carrying capacity of the Class 158s. Future partnership plans will see Porterbrook working with the Strategic Rail Authority and ScotRail to deliver equipment upgrades so as to further improve train reliability on the Iron Road to Whisky Country.

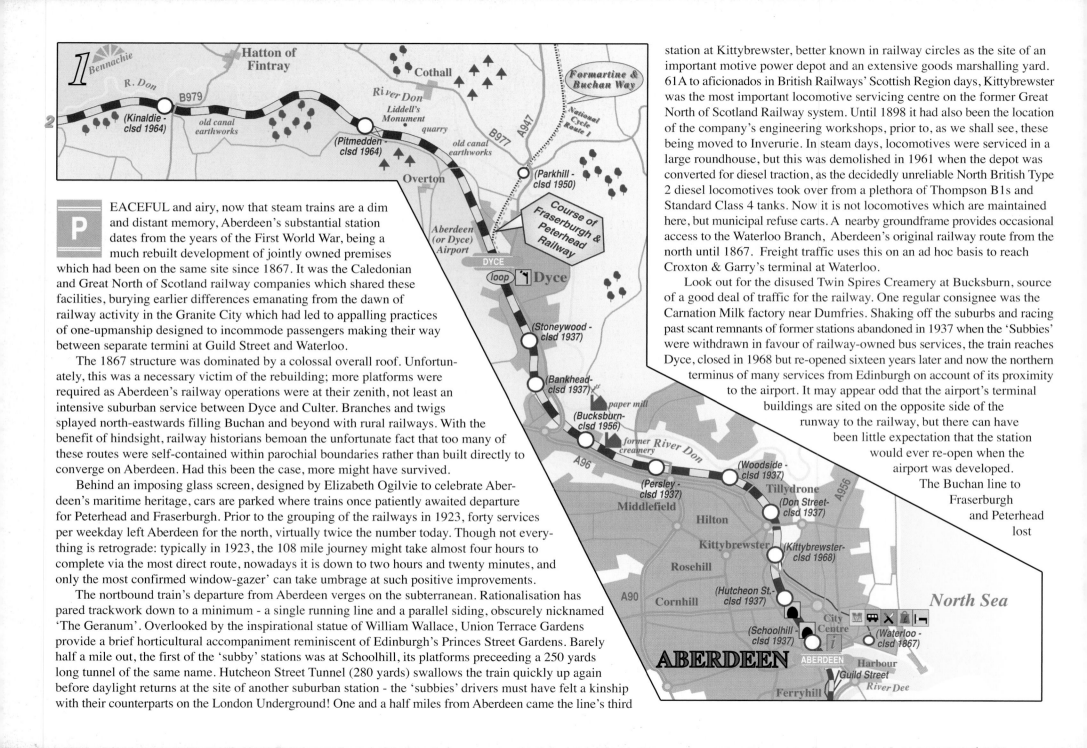

PEACEFUL and airy, now that steam trains are a dim and distant memory, Aberdeen's substantial station dates from the years of the First World War, being a much rebuilt development of jointly owned premises which had been on the same site since 1867. It was the Caledonian and Great North of Scotland railway companies which shared these facilities, burying earlier differences emanating from the dawn of railway activity in the Granite City which had led to appalling practices of one-upmanship designed to incommode passengers making their way between separate termini at Guild Street and Waterloo.

The 1867 structure was dominated by a colossal overall roof. Unfortunately, this was a necessary victim of the rebuilding; more platforms were required as Aberdeen's railway operations were at their zenith, not least an intensive suburban service between Dyce and Culter. Branches and twigs splayed north-eastwards filling Buchan and beyond with rural railways. With the benefit of hindsight, railway historians bemoan the unfortunate fact that too many of these routes were self-contained within parochial boundaries rather than built directly to converge on Aberdeen. Had this been the case, more might have survived.

Behind an imposing glass screen, designed by Elizabeth Ogilvie to celebrate Aberdeen's maritime heritage, cars are parked where trains once patiently awaited departure for Peterhead and Fraserburgh. Prior to the grouping of the railways in 1923, forty services per weekday left Aberdeen for the north, virtually twice the number today. Though not everything is retrograde: typically in 1923, the 108 mile journey might take almost four hours to complete via the most direct route, nowadays it is down to two hours and twenty minutes, and only the most confirmed window-gazer' can take umbrage at such positive improvements.

The nortbound train's departure from Aberdeen verges on the subterranean. Rationalisation has pared trackwork down to a minimum - a single running line and a parallel siding, obscurely nicknamed 'The Geranum'. Overlooked by the inspirational statue of William Wallace, Union Terrace Gardens provide a brief horticultural accompaniment reminiscent of Edinburgh's Princes Street Gardens. Barely half a mile out, the first of the 'subby' stations was at Schoolhill, its platforms preceeding a 250 yards long tunnel of the same name. Hutcheon Street Tunnel (280 yards) swallows the train quickly up again before daylight returns at the site of another suburban station - the 'subbies' drivers must have felt a kinship with their counterparts on the London Underground! One and a half miles from Aberdeen came the line's third

station at Kittybrewster, better known in railway circles as the site of an important motive power depot and an extensive goods marshalling yard. 61A to aficionados in British Railways' Scottish Region days, Kittybrewster was the most important locomotive servicing centre on the former Great North of Scotland Railway system. Until 1898 it had also been the location of the company's engineering workshops, prior to, as we shall see, these being moved to Inverurie. In steam days, locomotives were serviced in a large roundhouse, but this was demolished in 1961 when the depot was converted for diesel traction, as the decidedly unreliable North British Type 2 diesel locomotives took over from a plethora of Thompson B1s and Standard Class 4 tanks. Now it is not locomotives which are maintained here, but municipal refuse carts. A nearby groundframe provides occasional access to the Waterloo Branch, Aberdeen's original railway route from the north until 1867. Freight traffic uses this on an ad hoc basis to reach Croxton & Garry's terminal at Waterloo.

Look out for the disused Twin Spires Creamery at Bucksburn, source of a good deal of traffic for the railway. One regular consignee was the Carnation Milk factory near Dumfries. Shaking off the suburbs and racing past scant remnants of former stations abandoned in 1937 when the 'Subbies' were withdrawn in favour of railway-owned bus services, the train reaches Dyce, closed in 1968 but re-opened sixteen years later and now the northern terminus of many services from Edinburgh on account of its proximity to the airport. It may appear odd that the airport's terminal buildings are sited on the opposite side of the runway to the railway, but there can have been little expectation that the station would ever re-open when the airport was developed.

The Buchan line to Fraserburgh and Peterhead lost

its passenger trains in 1965 and freight in 1979 and 1970 respectively. This section of the Great North of Scotland empire formed a characterful collection of lines, notable for its busy fish traffic. On 2nd July 1918, no less than sixteen fish specials were laid on in connection with the herring trade. In the autumn extra passenger trains were operated between Fraserburgh, Peterhead and Great Yarmouth as fishing workers migrated to East Anglia in pursuit of the shoals of 'silver darlings'.

From Ellon, 13 miles north of Dyce, a branch was somewhat optimistically constructed to Boddam. For a brief halcyon period it served the GNoSR's own magnificent hotel at Cruden Bay - a railway inspired resort where no expense was spared in lavish catering. An electric tram conveyed passengers from the railway station to the hotel, and remarkably survives in preservation at the Grampian Transport Museum, Alford (Tel: 01975 562292). Had the hotel been built in Bournemouth, Torquay, or perhaps *even* Cullen, it might have proved more durable. When World War II broke out its Italian chef was interned, whilst the massive building was requisitioned by the military and demolished after the war.

The junction at Dyce lay to the south of the station, and the Buchan line had its own pair of platforms, the fish & chip shop occupies part of the old station buildings. Not all is lost, however, for the trackbed - twenty-three miles of it to Maud, followed by a further fifteen to Fraserburgh and thirteen to Peterhead respectively - has been restored as a public footpath, cycleway and bridleway called the *Formartine & Buchan Way*. National Cycle Route 1 (and, indeed, the international North Sea Cycle Route) uses the Way as far as Newmachar, so, in theory at any rate, you can cycle from Dyce to Denmark! Railway romantics may, regrettably, no longer be able to travel behind an exiled Holden 'Hiker' in a GNoS composite carriage to Udny to see the concrete mansion at Tillycorthie, or Strichen for the stone circle, but they can

transmogrify themselves in their fertile imaginations into a train of similar pedigree, pedalling furiously through cuttings and on embankments to Maud where a small museum (Tel: 01771 622906) celebrates the railway's rich heritage.

The Aberdeen line shakes off urbanisation beyond the Dyce ring-road, entering pleasant countryside through which the River Don meanders with much charm. At eighty miles, the Don is Scotland's sixth lengthiest river. Near Cothall it twists through a picturesque gorge. Liddell's Monument commemorates one Duncan Liddell, a 16th century Rector of the Julian University in Rome and Physician to the Court of Brunswick.

Keen-eyed students of transport history may well have their suspicions aroused by tell-tale earthworks which appear from time to time beside the railway between Dyce and the outskirts of Inverurie. U-shaped and a couple of dozen feet wide, they can hardly be the track bed of a dismantled railway. In fact, they are the remnants of the Aberdeenshire Canal, an inland waterway opened in 1805 and probably unique in its seasonal use, little point being deemed sensible in attempting to operate it through the freezing winters of Scotland's north-east! The canal was nineteen miles long and featured seventeen locks, so that a voyage along its full length took four or five hours. Nevertheless this was an improvement on the roads of the period, and for a number of years the canal even carried a passenger service with iron built 'fly-boats' alongside wooden barges heavily laden with agricultural produce and granite. In financial difficulty during the deep economic depression which followed the Napoleonic Wars, the canal company were only too happy to sell out to the Great North of Scotland Railway who set about incorporating its straighter lengths for their own use. Rhododendrons grow on the ruined platforms at Kinaldie.

Quiet Flows The Don
With the outline of Bennachie in the distance, an Aberdeen bound train passes the meandering river south-east of Kintore.

Inverurie snapshots - *Top left:* a Class 158 waits to leave with a train for Aberdeen; *top right:* exterior view of the station building; *lower left:* a loaded timber wagon awaits collection; *lower right:* interior view of waiting room and booking hall.

MORE remnants of the old canal can be seen on the approach to Kintore, its towpath is evident as well. Look out also for some championship-winning Clydesdale horses in fields neighbouring the railway. Not only commuters bemoan the fact that Kintore no longer has a railway station, for it is an historic burgh notable for its handsome 18th century Town House. From time to time initiatives are proposed to re-open Kintore station as part of a Cross-Aberdeen local service.

Kintore was the junction for the Alford Valley Railway, a sixteen mile branch plagued with construction difficulties, not least the Bacchanalian tendencies of its itinerant workforce. Oh but what mellifluous station names - Kenmay, Monymusk, Tillyfourie, Whitehouse; and even a private siding known as Paradise! But poetry couldn't prevent it from losing money, and its passenger services were withdrawn in 1950, though goods pottered along its rickety track for another sixteen years. It can be explored by road, of course, a worthwhile day out, especially if combined with a visit to the transport museum at Alford.

Esparto grass used to be unloaded at Aberdeen Harbour and taken in railway wagons to the paper mills at Bucksburn, Dyce and Inverurie. Now there are only rusting sidings beside the mill at Port Elphinstone, a suburb of Inverurie deriving its name from the old canal. Crossing the River Don, the railway enters Inverurie, a former railway town where even the local Highland League football club are known as 'The Locos'! The Great North of Scotland Railway opened their works at Inverurie at the beginning of the 20th century and it remained in business until 1969, dominating the town's economy for the greater part of that period. The last steam locomotive to be repaired here was none other than the A4 streamliner *Sir Nigel Gresley*. By way of consolation, a good proportion of the works' premises remain in use by other industrial concerns. Inverurie station dates from the opening of the works and is well worth alighting to see. Its beautiful wood-panelled waiting room is adorned by archive photographs of the works in its heyday. Timber traffic continues to use the sidings at Inverurie and the movement of trains is controlled from a now unnecessarily large timber built signal cabin.

The River Urie accompanies the line out of Inverurie, and abandoned bridge piers can be seen where the Old Meldrum line - closed to passengers as early as 1931 (despite savings in cost associated with the introduction of steam railcars), though retained for freight until 1966 - curved eastwards. The Battle of Harlaw occurred at the violent end of an acrimonious dispute between the Lord of the Isles and the Earl of Mar in 1411, and is generally considered to have been one of the bloodiest conflicts ever fought on Scottish soil. Another long forgotten branch left the main line at Inveramsay. This was the Turriff and Macduff line, an impecunious affair even by north-east Scotland standards. According to that doyen of Scottish railway history writers, John Thomas, its directors considered running trains before the track was ballasted, so desperate were they for income. The company spent £1,500 on fencing alone against passenger receipts of £270! The controversial Scottish educationalist, R.F.Mackenzie, spent his childhood at Wartle, the first stop down the line, where his father was stationmaster for a number of years. In his final book, *A Search for Scotland*, he makes a number of references to the railways of the district, and the inherent sense of community they engendered. He relates the story of an engine driver, asked to retire at seventy, who responded: 'If I had thoct it wasna to be a permanent job, I would never have ta'en it on.' Pitcaple Castle is a 15th century Z-plan tower house. Mary Queen of Scots dined here in September 1562 and planted a thorn tree beneath which her great-grandson, Charles II, danced in 1650. The tree lived until 1856 and was succeeded by a maple planted by Queen Mary in 1923. Pitcaple's timber station houses a football memorabilia shop - Tel: 01467 681666.

Whiteford
Pitcaple Castle
Mill of Durno
A96
Course of Macduff Railway
(Pitcaple - clsd 1968)
(Inveramsay - clsd 1951)
Course of Old Meldrum Railway
Chapel of Garioch
Harlaw House
B9001
(Lethenty - clsd 1931)
Stone Circle
Battle of Harlaw 1411
Inveramsay
Monument
River Urie
B9170
Bennachie
Dilly Hill 478ft
Inverurie Locos F.C.
Former Railway Works
INVERURIE (loop)
Inverurie
i
Keith Hall
motte & bailey remains
Port Elphinstone
River Don
B993
Don Viaduct
Bruce's Camp
Kinkell Church paper mill
B993
Course of Alford Railway
A96
River Don
(Kintore - clsd 1964)
Kintore
B977
Tuach Hill 273ft
old canal earthworks

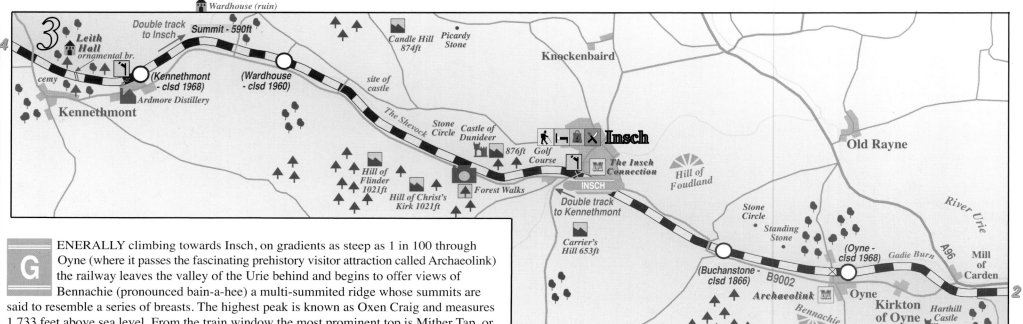

ENERALLY climbing towards Insch, on gradients as steep as 1 in 100 through Oyne (where it passes the fascinating prehistory visitor attraction called Archaeolink) the railway leaves the valley of the Urie behind and begins to offer views of Bennachie (pronounced bain-a-hee) a multi-summited ridge whose summits are said to resemble a series of breasts. The highest peak is known as Oxen Craig and measures 1,733 feet above sea level. From the train window the most prominent top is Mither Tap, or 'mother top', a granite crowned, nippled breast 1,698 feet high. Bennachie lies close to the hearts of Aberdeenshire folk. It is the first sighting of land for Aberdonian fishermen on their way back into port. A folk song celebrates it and the Gadie burn: "Oh! gin I were far Gadie rins, at the back o Bennachie" and its tune is the regimental march of the Gordon Highlanders. Harthill Castle dates from 1601 and was once the home of John Leith aka 'the violent laird'.

Smallest of settlements still served by a station on this route, Insch demonstrates how all twenty-first century village stations might appear were the world a perfect place. It may seem an oxymoron that this is Scotland's 'most passenger friendly unmanned station', but the fact is that the station building was restored by Railtrack in 1997 and suitable use sought for the premises. What could be more suitable than a lady kiltmaker and a small museum devoted to Insch's cultural, and railway past? The track doubles here under the watchful eye of a traditional signalbox dating from 1860, but recently refurbished and equipped with toilet facilities for the first time. Two of the incumbent signalmen are from interesting backgrounds - one is a former Squadron Leader who retired early from the forces to set up an archive of historic transport photographs, the other a classical music composer in his spare time and easily recognised by the fact that he usually wears a kilt to work.

All that remains of the medieval castle of Dunnideer is an arched tower astride a conical hill, 876ft above sea level. It's said to be the earliest authenticated tower house on the Scottish mainland, but the site may well have also been an Iron Age fortification, albeit an 'unfinished' one. The present ruin is all that remains of a substantial castle erected by Sir John de Balliol in the 13th century. His wife, Devorguila, founded Oxford's Balliol College in her husband's memory in 1269. Insch golf course was extended to eighteen holes in 1997. The earlier 9 hole

course was requisitioned during the Second World War for experimenting with grenades. Explosives are still tested on the slopes of Dunnideer, temporarily chasing the local herd of deer away from their fertile grazing grounds on its flanks.

Wardhouse station was built originally for the Gordons of Wardhouse, a Spanish Scots dynasty. Their grandiose property, ruined since 1952, broods on its hillside a mile to the west. King Alfonso XIIIth of Spain honeymooned here with his queen, Victoria Eugenia, in 1906, having survived an assassination attempt on his wedding day! A Pedro Carlos Gordon, known as the 'Mad Laird' is reputed to have raced the train from Wardhouse to Insch on horseback when the railway first arrived. His son, Juan Jose Gordon, held bull-fights in a specially constructed bull-ring in the grounds.

Crossing the summit of the line, Kennethmont is reached, its disused timber station an eerie *Marie Celeste*, on one interior wall of which a peeling poster informs passengers that their trains are about to be withdrawn and that W. Alexandra & Sons will provide a replacement bus. As the line singles again, it passes Teachers Ardmore Distillery which derives its water from the slopes of Knockandy Hill to the north. Opened in 1898, coal is still used to fire the stills, though sadly it no longer arrives by rail. The original steam plant and other historic artefacts are on display and the distillery can be visited on summer afternoons - Tel: 01464 831213. Leith Hall (1650) was given to the National Trust for Scotland in 1945. Among its treasures is a writing set presented by Bonnie Prince Charlie to one Andrew Raynes on the eve of Culloden. Tel: 01464 831216. The carriageway is borne over the railway on a handsome stone bridge with ornamental parapets.

The Quiet of a Country Station

A peaceful evening at Insch as a solitary passenger passes the time until the next Inverness train and a van speeds across the level crossing with Dunnideer in the distance.

Boogie-woogie in Strathbogie
The rhythm of the rails echoes a dance routine as a Class 158 unit makes its way towards Huntly beside the River Bogie.

HAVING crossed the watershed between the Urie and the Bogie, the line begins a sequence of falling gradients. 'Sting' may have sung about *Fields of Barley*, but here they are in reality, upholstering a luxuriant landscape of considerable charm. This railway doesn't go in for the histrionic scenic dramas of the West Highland or Kyle lines, but there's an understated beauty in its traverse of these broad, sunlit (metaphorically if not meteorologically) uplands which has a way of taking a lengthier lease of your topographic emotions than many a mountainous vista. And the railway contributes to this sensation in a perhaps unexpected manner, being the last line in Britain (other than restored lines preserved, so to speak, in aspic) to be accompanied by telegraph poles bearing insulators, carrying telegraphic wires which fall and rise in a trance-inducing manner, and your train often enhances this period feel by beating out a rhythm on the jointed track, as yet not fully equipped with long sections of welded rail. At one time the poles apparently carried up to a maximum of forty-eight insulators each, now they average between four and eight wires. Solely, then, is the rolling stock likely to be of modern aspect and, as you are - by definition - inside looking out, then you have every excuse for peeling back the years, and succumbing to a more gracious, less hurried era of rail travel.

The Water of Bogie becomes a close companion as the line arcs between the partially afforested summits of the Hill of Noth (to the west) and Knockandy Hill (to the east). Beyond the Hill of Noth (ablaze with yellow-flowering broom in early summer) you might sight the Tap o' Noth, a prominent cone shaped summit of 1,851ft. At the summit there are the remains of a substantial fortification. Possibly dating from as long ago as the 1st millennium BC, experts believe that there was a large oblong fort here with high stone walls reinforced with timber baulks. In the further distance stands The Buck of Cabrach, a cone shaped peak standing 2,368ft above sea level. Nowadays, Tap o' Noth is no longer intent on repelling visitors. Any reasonably fit walker can reach the top and it has also become a popular launch pad for hang gliders.

In common with Wardhouse, Gartly is another empty station building, though again those gilt-edged letters spell out its former role in local transport. The valley is steep-sided hereabouts and a by-road plunges down to cross the line by way of a level crossing protected by automatic half barriers.

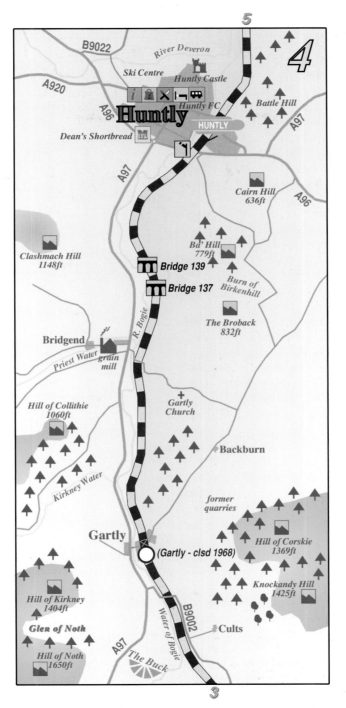

Farms in the vicinity bear evocative names such as Mains of Gartly, Mains of Kirkney, Mains of Collithie, but two name*less* masonry viaducts carry the railway over the watercourse which is now substantial enough to call itself the River Bogie. Under Clashmach Hill the train slows down for Huntly, a very likeable small town, birthplace of George MacDonald, the Victorian novelist and poet, friend of Lewis Carroll and hero of C.S. Lewis, perhaps best remembered for his 1886 children's classic *At The Back Of The North Wind*.

Timber traffic is still loaded by EWS at Huntly as market conditions demand. Several interesting buildings survive in the goods yard and it does not take too much imagination to picture how it must have looked in its busy heyday when all the freight to and from Huntly would have been handled here. The carriage of sheep and cattle would have been a particularly significant aspect of this traffic, given the proximity of the town's auction mart. On most days of the week a horse was used to move wagons about the yard, but on Wednesdays, when the mart was in full swing, a shunting engine would be sent down from Keith to cope with the extra traffic.

The railway reached Huntly, forty miles from Aberdeen in 1854. The original station was graced with an overall roof. In his seminal history of the Great North of Scotland Railway, H.A. Vallance paints a vivid picture of the opening ceremonies. Apparently preparations for the arrival of the inaugural train had brought sedate old Huntly almost to a standstill: 'At about twelve minutes past one o'clock, the long line of carriages drew slowly up to the platform (and) the people gave vent to their pent-up excitement in round upon round of deafening cheers'.

Regretably, the station's overall roof has gone, but regeneration by Railtrack has resulted in an attractive modern station building featuring reconstituted tiling on the roof with deep, weatherboarded eaves, a comfortable waiting room and a cheerful 'Cockney' stationmaster who 'would never go back'! Much of the timber loaded on to trains at Huntly comes from the vast Clashindarroch Forest to the west of the town. Previously the hills were bare and noted grouse moors. Huntly FC play in the Highland League at Christie Park. Formed in 1921, they hold the record for successive championships, being five time winners between 1993 and 1998.

BEYOND Huntly, the railway follows the valley of the River Deveron, a watercourse which rises on the remote north-facing shoulders of The Buck of Cabrach, before essaying a convoluted journey to the sea at Banff. Running parallel with the north-flowing river, the railway naturally heads downhill as far as the old station at Rothiemay, whereupon, exchanging the Deveron for its tributary, the River Isla, it begins to climb again. Substantial plantations of conifer trees lie to either side of the line, this section of which opened between Huntly and Keith in 1856. A five-arch skew viaduct had to be built to carry the line across the Deveron just short of Rothiemay station. Later this was rebuilt as the lattice-girder bridge in use today, in order that the track could be doubled. Now, of course, it is single again! The bases of the old masonry piers can still be discerned below to the east by hawk-eyed observers.

Forty-eight and a quarter miles from Aberdeen the line reaches CairnieJunction. Or rather it did, for Cairnie's ghost of an exchange platform resides in the past tens now. But what a wonderful place it must have been in its heyday, a self-contained station where passengers only alighted to change trains, and even that motive was paramountly the province of Keith and Dufftown folk bound to and from the coast, because at Cairnie trains were split or joined for railway operating expedience into through-running portions. Thus one could remain in one's carriage (always assuming you had ensconced yourself in the correct portion of the train) and be shunted appropriately into a train bound inland for Keith (where further shunting might well take place into portions bound most directly for Elgin via Mulben or involving further peregrinations through Dufftown and Craigallachie) or - most romantically of all - for the Moray Coast. Such arcane railway rites endured until the Dufftown and coastal lines fell victim to Beeching and closed in 1968. Contemporary witnesses, concerned with the struggle to save the coastal route, remain convinced that it was only lost at the last minute.

Nowadays you would need to be a railway detective in the mould of Sherlock Holmes or John Rebus to decipher any evidence of the existence of Cairnie Junction. Only a platelayers hut remains where there was formerly a lengthy island platform bordered by loops to facilitate the splitting and joining of trains. Aberdeen bound trains, arriving off the coastal route, were prone to run un-nervingly through the station on an outer loop, before appearing to stop and reconsider matters and then reverse into the platform to pick up the portion previously arrived from Keith and beyond. What a shame this picturesque line was forced to close. Its survival would have boosted tourism all along the Moray Coast. One interesting incident in its history concerned the capture of a trio of German spies (two men and one woman) who were landed from the sea at Buckie in 1940. Two of them attempted to catch a train at Portgordon station but aroused the suspicions of the station master and were promptly arrested. The third managed to reach Edinburgh by train before also being apprehended. The men were subsequently executed, but the woman survived the war and became a double agent!

Curving westwards, the remaining railway passes under the shadow of Little Balloch Hill and crosses the boundary between Aberdeenshire and Moray. To the north east there are good views of Knock Hill, a notable landmark for travellers on the old coast railway. Barely half a mile from Cairnie another abandoned station is encountered at Grange, the original junction for the Banff, Portsoy & Strathspey Railway opened in 1857. The branch to Banff - which diverged from the coastal route at the remote junction station of Tillynaught - closed in 1964, another regrettable casualty serving an important coastal town. Once again, it may have fared better had it not been built (like many GNoS routes) as a branch of a branch.

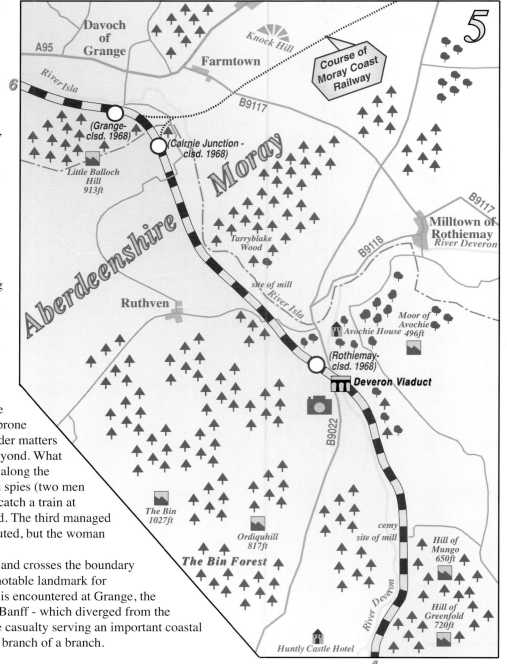

Bridge Over Peaceful Waters
Impressive engineering carries the line across
the River Deveron at Rothiemay.

Heart of Whisky Country 1

Slowing down on its approach to Keith from the south, a train for Inverness passes mountains of stored whisky casks beside the line. Knock Hill on the horizon.

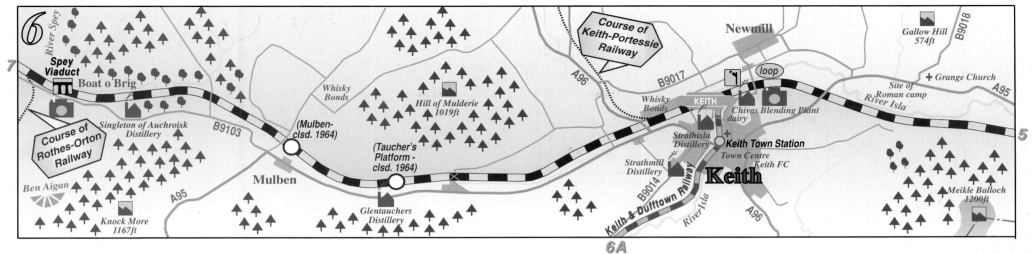

ENTLY, through Strathisla, the train runs up to Keith. To the south the valley side climbs steeply through forestry to the summit of Meikle Balloch. Northwards the landscape is flatter, being threaded by largely traffic innocent B roads heading for the coast and invoking an almost Irish sense of isolation. One James Gordon Bennett was born at Newmill in 1795, moving (like many compatriots) to Nova Scotia in 1819 and later the U.S.A. He found work as a journalist and founded the *New York Herald* in 1835, becoming as a result a very rich and famous man. But, if anything, it was his son, James Gordon Bennett Junior who was even better known. He took over ownership of the *Herald* in 1868 and lived in such a lavish and outrageous manner as to lend his name to a much used italicised expletive!

Watermeadows are suddenly exchanged for veritable mountains of whisky casks. This is certainly a sight to quicken the pulse of those partial to a 'wee dram', but there's an accompanying sadness to be felt by railway supporters that none of the traffic associated with the whisky business either arrives or departs by train. In fact it was here at Keith the last regular use of rail transport was employed by the whisky trade. Chivas Regal had adapted the former GNoS engine shed (south of the line, at the east end of the station) and converted it into a blending and storage plant. They used tanks attached to flat wagons to convey whisky to a bottling plant at Dalmuir near Glasgow. Everything went smoothly until British Rail declared the cost of working the wagons out to Dalmuir 'uneconomic'! The GNoS goods shed remains intact, decaying machinery and rusty sidings emphasising lost traffics: arsenic free anthracite from South Wales for the distilleries; palleted bags of fertilizer for the barley fields; seed potatoes bound for Portugal which had to be loaded on frost-free days, grain bound for export via Teesport; rock salt for melting ice from Grampian roads.

Keith station - formerly known as Keith Junction to distinguish it from Keith Town on the GNoS Speyside line - once had quite a complex layout of trackwork. However, all this has been rationalised into a single running line with a loop located to the east of the station. Of the station's other four platforms, two were east-facing bays, one a west-facing bay for Highland services, whilst the other through platform catered for Speyside trains. This remains in place, still used by a morning Aberdeen to Keith and return working.

Now in what was Highland Railway territory, the train pulls away past former woollen mills which supplied vast quantities of blankets for the British Army during the Great War. Further evidence of the whisky industry's importance to the local economy comes in the shape of huge bonded warehouses bordering the line, emphasising the need for security while the whisky is maturing - only the angels being allowed to share the minute percentage which is lost through evaporation! The Keith to Portessie line was opened by the Highland Railway in 1884, largely stimulated by competition for the trade in fish. Each herring season fast fish trains clattered over its tracks on their way from Buckie to various destinations south of the border. But, steeply graded and tightly curved, it proved a difficult line to work and was abandoned during the First World War when a portion of its track was requisitioned by the Admiralty. Eventually it was reinstated by the LMS, though apparently never used.

Mileposts on the north side of the track measure the distance from Forres as the line climbs to a summit of just over four hundred feet above sea level at the site of Taucher's Platform, once provided for workers at the adjacent Glentauchers Distillery. Beyond Mulben the railway plunges downhill at 1 in 60 into a dense belt of woodland before emerging to cross the River Spey on a huge steel girder bridge which replaced an earlier wrought iron structure in 1906. Keep your eyes peeled for a curious little row of dog kennels tucked below the north side of the line on the east bank of the river. The peerless Spey flows majestically below, nearing the end of its almost hundred mile journey to the sea. In days gone by the river's strong current was employed to float logs down to the shipbuilding yards at Kingston on the coast. A shortlived connecting line ran between Orton and Rothes, but you can still discern its shallow earthworks sloping across a field to the south of the line west of its crossing of the Spey. Opened in 1858, as part of the Morayshire Railway, it was rendered obsolete when the GNoS reached Elgin from Rothes. It was abandoned in 1866 but the track wasn't lifted for over forty years.

WHAT a wonderful survival the Keith & Dufftown Railway is! Like the coastal route, it also lost its passenger services in one fell swoop on the 6th of May 1968 (typically as the summer season was getting into swing!), but a residual freight service between Keith Junction and a new grain terminal (whose silos still survive) at Dufftown saved some eleven miles of splendidly scenic track from being dismantled. When, in the sadly all too common course of events, rail freight ceased using the line in the early 1980s, it was again redeemed, this time by an unlikely saviour in the shape of a regularly operated passenger excursion train called the 'Northern Belle'. Brainchild of the Aberdeen businessman, John Begg, it used high quality British Rail InterCity stock off the overnight London-Aberdeen service to provide a popular day trip from Aberdeen to Dufftown when it would otherwise have simply lain in a siding. The inclusive excursion package included a visit to a Dufftown distillery and meals on the train. Other charter trains used the line as well, and it enjoyed something of an Indian Summer until its infrastructure began to deteriorate, and Sectorisation of the railways as a precursor to Privatisation, introduced Byzantine accounting procedures which served only to make such operations appear unviable.

Yet again the line might easily have been lifted had not the Keith & Dufftown Railway Association been formed to take the route over as a private railway. By preservation standards, their progress has been rapid, and their achievement in re-opening the full length of the line was recognised by a top Railway Heritage Association award in 2002. Grants from Moray, Badenoch & Strathspey Enterprise and the European Regional Development Fund have speeded the group's progress, and their priority now is to reconnect with the main network at Keith Junction, so that lucrative excursion traffic (and perhaps freight also) may once again use the line.

In the meantime trains run to and from Keith Town where you would be hard pressed to differentiate between the association's brand new replica station building and its elegant, weatherboarded predecessor, unusual in its split level design, built to a typical Great North of Scotland Railway pattern in the 1880s. Here, one of the line's charmingly retro 1950s diesel multiple units will be waiting to embark on the forty minute ride to Dufftown. One prospective passenger was recently heard to derogatively remark: "But I go to work on a train like that *every* day!" Lucky man - the last Derby Lightweight Class 108 was actually withdrawn in 1993!

The railway climbs steadily from Keith up the narrowing valley of the River Isla. On its way out of town it passes Strathmill Distillery, still displaying a siding once used for bringing coal and grain inwards and casks of whisky out. Further industry in the shape of a bone works, or more vernacularly, a knacker's yard, follows before the train reaches the site of Auchindachy station, its building now in domestic use. Nearby, the Mill of Towie, though preserved,

is regretably not currently open to the public. At Towiemore a halt was provided to carry workers to an adjacent distillery, some of the premises survive in use as a works making stainless steel items.

The valley narrows and grows hillier and more swarthy as the half-way house of Drummuir is approached. It would be a missed opportunity not to alight here and explore this wayside station's bosky hinterland. There are several waymarked walks into the woods to be enjoyed, an organic walled garden, and the sweet little 19th century Kirk of Botriphnie to visit. Plenty, in fact, to do before rejoining the train for the remainder of the journey to Dufftown. In the old days there were sidings at Drummuir, kept busy with agricultural produce. The Association plan to reinstate them and add a small engine shed, for hopefully locomotive haulage will return to Strathisla in due course. Fumack, a 6th century saint, lived in the vicinity and is said to have blessed a local well. Some magic must have rubbed off, because the Kirk had only five ministers in two hundred and fifty years between 1680 and 1930, and their longevity of tennure was put down to the medicinal properties of the water! The mock battlements of 19th century Drummuir Castle peep over the tree-tops to watch your train amble through the valley. One of its past owners was far from impressed, complaining that it was vulgar and pretentious and that an unnecessarily large number of servants was required on account of the length of its passages!

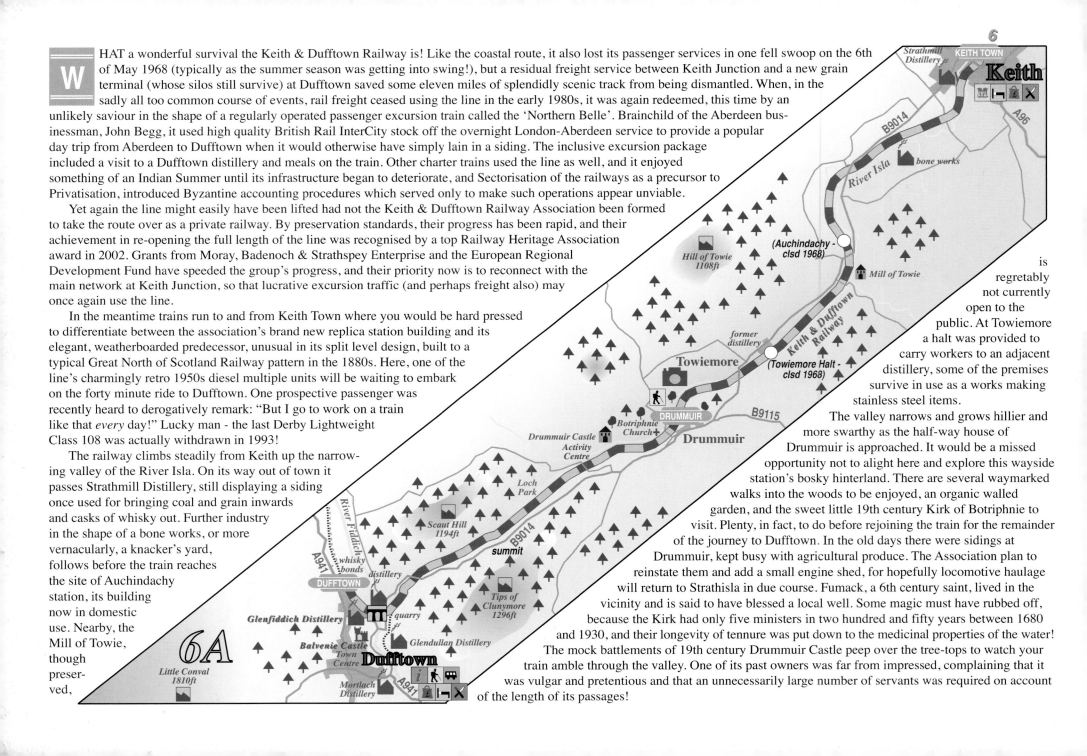

Now the railway enters its most beautiful stretch as it runs through a precipitously sided valley beside the waters of a man-made loch. Originally this marshy ground was the source of the River Isla. Early in the 19th century the laird of Drummuir had it drained, but his successor made a more inspired contribution to the landscape, creating the sinuous length of water encountered today, a popular provider of recreation for anglers, watersports enthusiasts and exuberantly noisy school groups. During the Second World War there was a sawmill beside the loch and a narrow gauge railway was laid to carry felled trees to the mill from adjacent forestry plantations. Lewis Morrison Grant - 'the northern Keats' was born in a cottage overlooking the loch in 1872, but died tragically young in 1893, never fulfilling his early promise. Just beyond the western end of the loch the line reaches its summit. In steam days, firemen on the footplate of D40s and B1s would have heaved a sigh of relief at this point and rested on their laurels for the steep 1 in 60 run down into Dufftown. Leaning out of the cab, they might have seen otters and orchids, and so might you!

Passing some quarry workings, and the trackbed of a branch which once led down to the Glendullan Distillery, the train slows to cross the River Fiddich on the line's most imposing engineering work, a double arch viaduct, 60ft feet high. Whichever way you're looking from the train, there is interest in the view: to the south Balvenie Castle overlooks the railway; to the north, on the riverside stand Balvenie and Parkmore distilleries. It is with regret that the train slows to a halt at Dufftown station - you want the journey to go on and on! Until 1968 it did, continuing to Craigellachie, Rothes and Elgin through glorious countryside, an even more picturesque way of getting from Keith to Elgin than the Highland Railway's more direct route which ScotRail use. Consolation, of a kind, comes from being able to pace out the old railway's course on foot through Glen Fiddich on the *Spey Way*.

Dufftown is the administrative headquarters of the Keith & Dufftown Association. The station is a typical GNoSR structure, right down to the gold-leafed name adorning the glass above the entrance to the booking hall. Inside you'll find some interesting exhibits, a small souvenir shop, and friendly advice on how best to spend your time in Dufftown. In the bay platform a restored British Railways Mk1 carriage has been converted into *The Buffer Stop* restaurant and cafe. Beyond the end of the platform, a preserved Class 140 diesel unit (precursor of the often maligned four-wheeled 'Pacers' which proliferate on various suburban routes and branchlines south of the border) has been put out to graze as a 'reading room' and place to contemplate the highs and lows of railway history. The railways of north-East Scotland may be a shadow of their pre-Beeching selves, but the Keith & Dufftown's star is in the ascent. Keep an eye on its progress!

Heart of Whisky Country 2
A Keith & Dufftown 'heritage' diesel unit crosses the
River Isla near Auchindachy.

Stately swans on Loch Oire near Lhanbryde, the railway runs through the trees behind the loch.

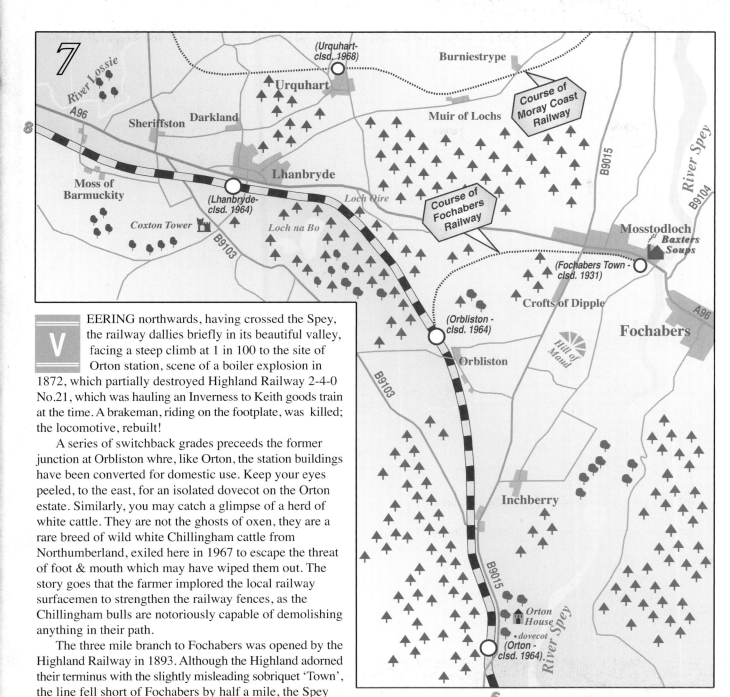

Map labels:
(Urquhart- clsd. 1968)
Burniestrype
River Lossie
A96
Urquhart
Sheriffston   Darkland
Muir of Lochs
Course of Moray Coast Railway
B9015
River Spey
B9104
Lhanbryde
Moss of Barmuckity
(Lhanbryde- clsd. 1964)
Loch Oire
Course of Fochabers Railway
Coxton Tower
B9103
Loch na Bo
Mosstodloch
Baxters Soups
(Fochabers Town - clsd. 1931)
Crofts of Dipple
Fochabers
(Orbliston - clsd. 1964)
Orbliston
Hill of Maud
A96
Inchberry
B9103
B9015
Orton House
dovecot
(Orton - clsd. 1964)
River Spey

VEERING northwards, having crossed the Spey, the railway dallies briefly in its beautiful valley, facing a steep climb at 1 in 100 to the site of Orton station, scene of a boiler explosion in 1872, which partially destroyed Highland Railway 2-4-0 No.21, which was hauling an Inverness to Keith goods train at the time. A brakeman, riding on the footplate, was killed; the locomotive, rebuilt!

A series of switchback grades preceeds the former junction at Orbliston whre, like Orton, the station buildings have been converted for domestic use. Keep your eyes peeled, to the east, for an isolated dovecot on the Orton estate. Similarly, you may catch a glimpse of a herd of white cattle. They are not the ghosts of oxen, they are a rare breed of wild white Chillingham cattle from Northumberland, exiled here in 1967 to escape the threat of foot & mouth which may have wiped them out. The story goes that the farmer implored the local railway surfacemen to strengthen the railway fences, as the Chillingham bulls are notoriously capable of demolishing anything in their path.

The three mile branch to Fochabers was opened by the Highland Railway in 1893. Although the Highland adorned their terminus with the slightly misleading sobriquet 'Town', the line fell short of Fochabers by half a mile, the Spey being deemed too wide at this point to justify the expense

of a suitably lengthy bridge. Perhaps this explains the early demise of passenger services in 1931, that and the unfortunate fact that connections were not always exactly well-synchronised with main line trains at the junction. Nowadays Fochabers is best known as the location of Baxters soup factory and is a very popular stopover on most tourist trails. Who knows, had the branch not been ripped up after freight stopped being carried over it in 1966, it might have survived to become a showcase, steam-operated shuttle associated with Baxters visitor centre.

The GNoS once also had a station called Fochabers, but it was even more risibly distant from the town, a good four miles in fact, and later they rather more realistically let it be known as Spey Bay. It was on their Moray Coast line whose melancholy trackbed we last saw slinking away at Grange and Cairnie junctions. Hereabouts we've almost caught up with its arcing coastal itinerary, so cruelly and unnecessarily brought to an end in 1968. As the train runs down through forestry to Lhanbryde, the old coastal line's remnants lie only a country mile to the north in the vicinity of Urquhart, a wayside station which ironically kept its passenger services four years longer than the likes of Lhanbryde and Orbliston. Once upon a time the Highland and Great North of Scotland railways must have vied with great rivalry for the trade of farmers in the district, even down to the despatch and collection of milk churns. The surfacemen hereabouts often kept a croft to supplement their earnings. They were allowed to harvest the hay which grew on the embankments on their length.

A worthwhile project for another day would be to follow the remains of the Moray Coast railway along what really is an 'undiscovered' coastline characterised by charming fishing villages and remote, sandy bays overlooked by precipitous cliffs. A highlight of such an expedition might be to walk across the remarkable Speymouth Viaduct at Garmouth, almost a thousand feet long in order to clear the river's delta-like flood plain, and dominated by a massive bowed central truss which can be seen for miles. For once where railway exploration is concerned, there is no requirement to trespass as the bridge has become host to the *Spey Way*.

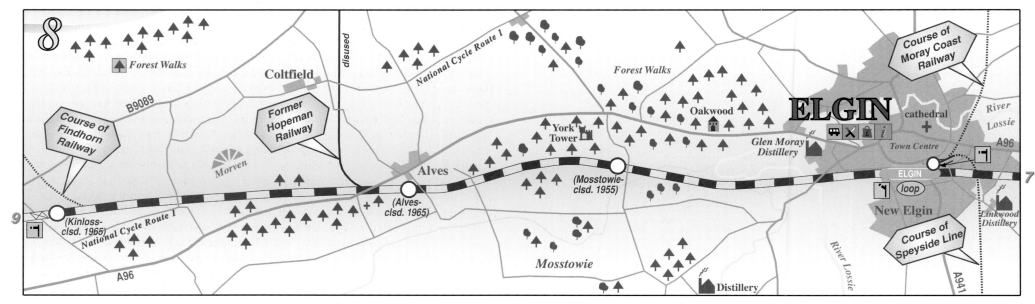

ISTORY hasn't been kind to Elgin's railways, and not only in as much that three of the four lines converging from the east have closed. Almost as great a sadness emanates from the putting aside of the Great North of Scotland Railway's swaggeringly flamboyant Scots Baronial station building of 1902, in favour of a numbly anodyne modern replacement on the site of the Highland Railway station, which remains in use a few hundred yards to the west. There are logical railway reasons for this - following the abandonment of the GNoSR's Moray Coast and Speyside lines, the more imposing of Elgin's side by side stations stood at a tangent to the only remaining tracks in use. In a more imaginative world the more charismatic station (which is Grade II listed) might have been retained by means of slewing the tracks in its favour: a Pullman carriage could have been stabled within its purlieus to administer Cordon Bleu Scots cuisine; the high vaulted booking hall could have been reserved for concerts, plays and exhibitions; the upper stories (crowned to the west by a conical towered corner turret) could have been sub-let for holiday accommodation; the east wing would have been ideal offices for the conveyancing and forwarding of freight trains, were any freight trains left to organise. Instead? Local businesses occupy the GNoS station and prospective rail passengers must share the comfort of strangers in a waiting room which reminds you despondently of a health clinic, right down to the chronic coughs of fellow passengers.

Being true to their Aberdonian origins, the Great North of Scotland did not habitually go in for lavish gestures, and the real reason for the exaggerated size of their station at Elgin was that it contained their administrative offices. R.F.Mackenzie perceived that 'it was something more than interest on their investments that shaped their instructions to the architect', and that 'they were ignoring the widely accepted idea that saving money

is the most important consideration'. Prior to Beeching, the station itself was a hive of activity, mirroring the splitting and joining of trains which went on at Cairnie Junction, but also serving as a terminus for the six mile branch from Lossiemouth, a fishing port which had grown with the siting of a Royal Naval Air Station on its doorstep. Ramsay MacDonald, Britain's first Labour Prime Minister, was born illegitimately in Lossiemouth in 1866. Between the wars the LNER had enthusiastically graced Lossiemouth with a through sleeping car service from London, the second lengthiest through carriage working in the country, beaten only by the Aberdeen-Penzance service. The windswept coastal terminus was notable in that a bell used to signal departure of the trains rather than a whistle. The quarter of an hour ride to Elgin lay across a particularly beautiful landscape of open, heather-clad moorlands sprinkled with pine trees and conifers and flatlands drained by the Spynie Canal. Typically, the branch passenger train would consist of two or three elderly carriages and a GNoSR 4-4-0, little changing when the North British Type 2 diesels took over until closure came sadly in 1964. A feature of the branch was its 'leave' trains, lengthy specials run for the benefit of the Naval Air Station.

No sooner have westbound trains apparently shaken off the dust of Elgin than they judder to a halt again. No one's been left behind, the driver's side window is down and he's collecting a token for the single line section to Forres, another welcome aspect of this admirably traditional rail route. The signal cabin is overlooked by the pagoda tower of an abandoned distillery. Crossing the River Lossie - which rises on Carn Kitty above Glen Trevie, twenty miles to the south - the railway traverses an area of low-lying heathland overlooked from the north by an octagonal, three storey folly called the York Tower erected in 1827 in memory of the Grand Old Duke of York. Masked by trees from the railway

Elgin's former GNoSR station: the Scot's Baronial exterior.

miles from the junction in the 1960s, retaining freight use until recent times and, as you will see, the track remains in situ, dreaming of its next trainload of grain.

Alves station enjoys a new lease of life as a private house. Clustered about it are other ex railway workers' cottages formerly provided for station staff, signalmen and surfacemen. There was even a communal washhouse! In its heyday the goods yard was busy with livestock, timber, coal and grain. More specifically, carrots were despatched for canning in Dundee, sugar beet went to Cupar, and milk went to Nairn and Inverness. Each autumn sheep arrived from less hospitable northern districts for wintering in Alves and districts comparatively mild climes. In the 1960s, when Prince Charles was attending nearby Gordonstoun School, the Royal Train would occasionally be stabled at Alves. If you can manage to look in both directions simultaneously, you may catch a glimpse on the south side of the line of the parish church of Alves - someway removed from its village - an interesting classical style building dating from 1878.

Less resilient than the Hopeman branch, the Findhorn Railway carried passengers for merely eight years beyond its opening in 1861, and even freight was abandoned before the end of the 19th century. Any remaining earthworks were obliterated by the construction of the RAF aerodrome here in April, 1939. Nowadays Findhorn has become a popular resort and a narrow gauge railway, laid ideally around the lovely shoreline of Findhorn Bay to Forres, would undoubtedly prove a popular and useful attraction.

traveller's view, motorists on the A96 encounter the eccentric Oakwood Motel dating from 1932, a rustic, log-built structure inspired by its builder's visit to Canada. It's a cafe and restaurant now with - appropriately enough - a sideline in curios. Were Mosstowie's remote station still intact, you could detrain here and visit the motel and the York Tower. It seems incredible that it stayed open as late as 1955 - perhaps the monks of Pluscarden Abbey, five miles to the south, had sung plainsong for it. The flat, boggy landscape which the railway traverses has an odd appeal all its own. In the past folk from Elgin would come out here to dig peat for fuel; a good deal of draining had to be done to make the land more suitable for farming.

Alves was the junction for the Hopeman branch, opened as far as Burghead Pier for the fish trade three days before Christmas in 1862 and extended along the coast to Hopeman thirty years later. Burghead-caught fish enjoyed a high reputation for quantity and quality; halibut the height of a tall man regularly being landed in the local catch. The Highland Railway altruistically provided free passes for fisherwomen to travel inland with creels of fresh fish to sell in the rural hinterland. With finely tuned commercial sensibilities, they returned to the coast with fresh vegetables for sale! Passenger trains operated along the seven mile branch until withdrawn by the LMS in the face of bus competition in 1931. Freight continued, however, and a massive new malting plant was constructed a couple of

Elgin's former GNoSR station: the splendid interior.

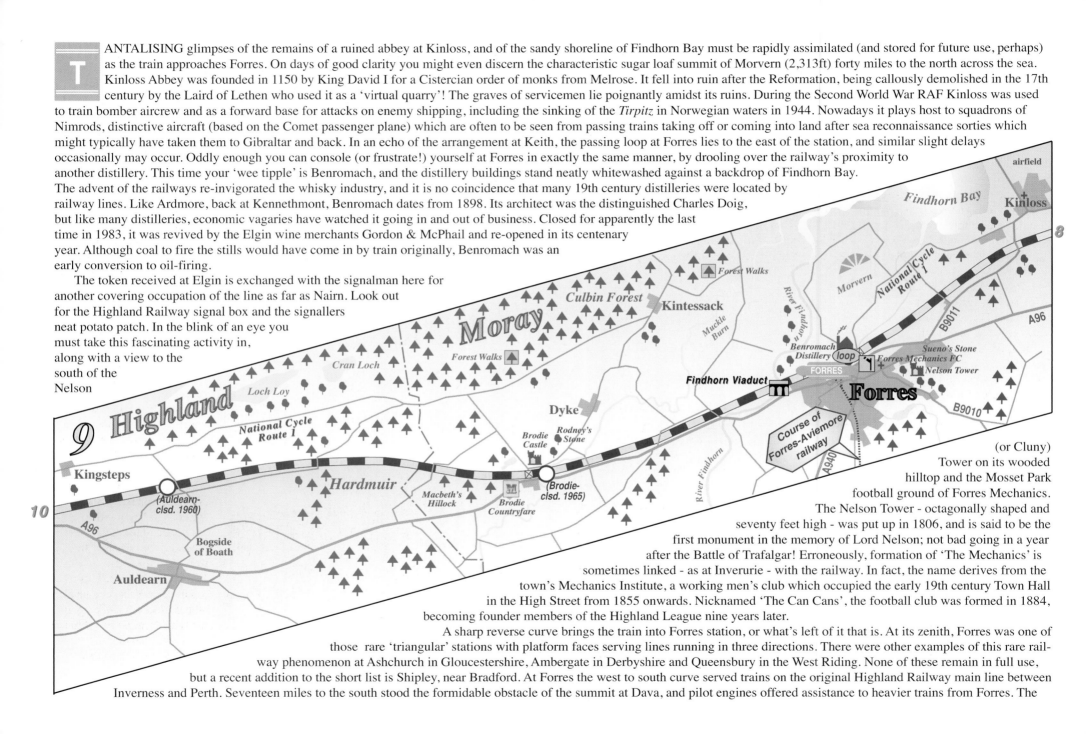

TANTALISING glimpses of the remains of a ruined abbey at Kinloss, and of the sandy shoreline of Findhorn Bay must be rapidly assimilated (and stored for future use, perhaps) as the train approaches Forres. On days of good clarity you might even discern the characteristic sugar loaf summit of Morvern (2,313ft) forty miles to the north across the sea. Kinloss Abbey was founded in 1150 by King David I for a Cistercian order of monks from Melrose. It fell into ruin after the Reformation, being callously demolished in the 17th century by the Laird of Lethen who used it as a 'virtual quarry'! The graves of servicemen lie poignantly amidst its ruins. During the Second World War RAF Kinloss was used to train bomber aircrew and as a forward base for attacks on enemy shipping, including the sinking of the *Tirpitz* in Norwegian waters in 1944. Nowadays it plays host to squadrons of Nimrods, distinctive aircraft (based on the Comet passenger plane) which are often to be seen from passing trains taking off or coming into land after sea reconnaissance sorties which might typically have taken them to Gibraltar and back. In an echo of the arrangement at Keith, the passing loop at Forres lies to the east of the station, and similar slight delays occasionally may occur. Oddly enough you can console (or frustrate!) yourself at Forres in exactly the same manner, by drooling over the railway's proximity to another distillery. This time your 'wee tipple' is Benromach, and the distillery buildings stand neatly whitewashed against a backdrop of Findhorn Bay. The advent of the railways re-invigorated the whisky industry, and it is no coincidence that many 19th century distilleries were located by railway lines. Like Ardmore, back at Kennethmont, Benromach dates from 1898. Its architect was the distinguished Charles Doig, but like many distilleries, economic vagaries have watched it going in and out of business. Closed for apparently the last time in 1983, it was revived by the Elgin wine merchants Gordon & McPhail and re-opened in its centenary year. Although coal to fire the stills would have come in by train originally, Benromach was an early conversion to oil-firing.

The token received at Elgin is exchanged with the signalman here for another covering occupation of the line as far as Nairn. Look out for the Highland Railway signal box and the signallers neat potato patch. In the blink of an eye you must take this fascinating activity in, along with a view to the south of the Nelson

(or Cluny) Tower on its wooded hilltop and the Mosset Park football ground of Forres Mechanics. The Nelson Tower - octagonally shaped and seventy feet high - was put up in 1806, and is said to be the first monument in the memory of Lord Nelson; not bad going in a year after the Battle of Trafalgar! Erroneously, formation of 'The Mechanics' is sometimes linked - as at Inverurie - with the railway. In fact, the name derives from the town's Mechanics Institute, a working men's club which occupied the early 19th century Town Hall in the High Street from 1855 onwards. Nicknamed 'The Can Cans', the football club was formed in 1884, becoming founder members of the Highland League nine years later.

A sharp reverse curve brings the train into Forres station, or what's left of it that is. At its zenith, Forres was one of those rare 'triangular' stations with platform faces serving lines running in three directions. There were other examples of this rare railway phenomenon at Ashchurch in Gloucestershire, Ambergate in Derbyshire and Queensbury in the West Riding. None of these remain in full use, but a recent addition to the short list is Shipley, near Bradford. At Forres the west to south curve served trains on the original Highland Railway main line between Inverness and Perth. Seventeen miles to the south stood the formidable obstacle of the summit at Dava, and pilot engines offered assistance to heavier trains from Forres. The single platform serving the east to south curve was apparently used just twice a day by a service which ran through from Glasgow to Aberdeen via Aviemore. Now just one platform remains in use, though happily the station is still staffed, its solitary ScotRail employee occupying the ticket office of a brick station building of austere 1954 provenance which would not have looked out of place in Rickmansworth or Staines. The former eastbound platform is backed by a high wall which provides a viewing gallery for Forres's local crow population. Note the zero milepost installed on the trackbed now. This marks the commencement of the Highland Railway's route to Keith, thirty miles away. West of Forres the mileposts are part of the original Highland main line from Perth via Aviemore and Dava, counting up from 120 to 144 at Inverness. Among the famous sons of Forres was one Donald Smith who was born here in 1820. Better known by his assumed title of Lord Strathcona, he rose through the ranks of the Hudson Bay Company to become Canada's High Commissioner. The railway connection is that it was he who drove the final spike which ceremoniously completed the Canadian Pacific's traverse of the Rocky Mountains in 1885.

The railway climbs out of Forres and crosses the River Findhorn on an interesting viaduct built to the designs of Joseph Mitchell in 1858. It is a triple span of box girder style said to owe its inspiration to Robert Stephenson's tubular bridges for the Chester & Holyhead Railway in North Wales. Of engineering significance it may be, but its high wrought iron girders obscure the view! Mitchell was a native of Forres and had worked with Thomas Telford on the Caledonian Canal before following in his father John's footsteps as chief engineer in charge of Highland roads and bridges. Engineering obviously ran in the blood, for his grandson was none other than Reginald Mitchell, designer of the Spitfire fighter plane in World War Two.

Token Exchange at Forres

Culbin's massive forest stretches from Findhorn Bay to Nairn and is recognised as a Site of Special Scientific Interest. It occupies a once wild tract of land often inundated by the sea in centuries past. Before being planted with trees it was known as the Scottish Sahara! The Forestry Commission acquired it in 1921 and set about stabilising the sand by tree planting using a mixture of Scots and Corsican pine. The remaining sand dunes are amongst the largest of their kind in Europe. Selective felling is carried out on a ten year cycle, permitting more daylight to penetrate the forest, encouraging flora and fauna to establish themselves in a bio-diverse manner.

Woods thick with rhododendrons lead to the old station at Brodie. There have been Brodies and Brodie for a thousand years, making the railway station's 'shelf-life' (1855-1965) seem just an ephemeral whim. If it had survived Beeching (who lacked the perspicacity to predict the economic benefits of tourism) you could alight now in style and visit Brodie Castle, an imposing 16th century tower house open to the public under the aegis of the National Trust for Scotland with the good offices of the twenty-fifth Brodie of Brodie. Similarly, tourists would also find the station a useful alighting point for the neighbouring Brodie Countryfare complex. The station house has 'Castle Brodie Station' engraved above the main entrance and nowadays offers bed & breakfast, a not entirely acceptable replacement for public transport.

Low-lying and pancake flat it may be, but there is a brooding atmosphere to this landscape which banishes any preconceptions about it being dull. Just before you cross the boundary between Moray and Highland an otherwise unremarkable mound to the south of the line bears the name Macbeth's Hillock. This is reputedly the 'blasted heath' where Macbeth came upon the witches as depicted in the opening scene of Shakespeare's 'Scottish Play'!

A BRIEF but intoxicating view of the Moray Firth offers itself to railway passengers as the train slows for Nairn, whilst a four arch viaduct carries the line across the river of the same name. On construction in 1856, the bridge was hailed enthusiastically by the local newspaper as 'a beautiful piece of work which will, in all probability, meet the gaze of many generations, for there is nothing in the north to compare with its elegance and symmetry'. Crossing it by early train, you might have glimpsed upstream, Nairn's womenfolk washing their household linens in the river.

Present day Nairn, with its high-spired church and towered town hall looks very appealing, and you shouldn't put up too much of a fight against being tempted to alight. Until 10th April, 2000 one could witness an enjoyable, if undeniably anachronistic, signalling ritual here. It had been a peculiarity of the Highland Railway to house its token instruments within station buildings whilst the lever frames to operate points and signals were to be found in signal cabins, usually located at one or other - but often both - ends of the station. The most convenient means of operation involved the signal person (for in latter years it was often a woman) cycling rapidly along the platform between the two boxes to effect each passage of a train. When trains passed here matters became even more complicated! Sadly, for railway enthusiasts and connoisseurs of the absurd, the East and West signal boxes at Nairn are boarded up now and used as storerooms, and only the token from Forres is exchanged; yet interestingly, the signallers of Nairn can be said to have swapped their bikes for a mouse, a computer 'mouse' that is, for their Westrace interlocking system is so far unique on Railtrack.

What does remain, however, is Nairn's exceedingly handsome station rebuilt from the 1855 original by the Highland Railway in 1885 in response to the town's burgeoning success as a resort. H plan in layout, it is reminiscent of Pitlochry and Dingwall, featuring the same pronounced Scots Tudor styling with crow-stepped gables and thistle finials. The main building in stone contrasts with an elegant timber waiting room with a bellcast roof on the opposite platform, now used, somewhat disconcertingly, only by eastbound trains. Also slightly puzzling, is the bridge on which the station and its platforms span the B9090, for on one side the girder was cast by Westwood Baillie & Co of London, whilst its counterpart bears the inscription Alex Findlay & Co of Motherwell!

Westbound trains depart past a big timber goods shed of typical Highland Railway pattern, beyond which there's a glimpse of the floodlights of Nairn County Football Club,

yet another team belonging to the Highland League. Formed in 1912, their ground is appropriately known as Station Park.

West of Nairn you are travelling along the route of the Inverness & Nairn Railway opened in 1855 and engineered by Joseph Mitchell. The overbridges are noticeably different from those east of Nairn, being particularly characterised by their rounded arches which they share in common with Mitchell's bridges on the Highland Main Line. The sea disappears behind the Carse of Delnies, but you can compensate by looking southwards in the direction of the wooded hills of Darnaway Forest. Although the land is low-lying, the gradients are not exactly imperceptible: a brief climb of 1 in 200 out of Nairn being followed by a half mile descent of 1 in 750, and then another upgrade of 1 in 250. Three miles to the south lies the famous Castle of Cawdor. It is said that its original 14th century owner had a dream in which he was urged to place his worldly treasures on the back of a donkey and follow wherever it led - modern building societies essentially employ the same tactic with those applying for a mortgage. Eventually it fell asleep under a hawthorn tree and Cawdor Castle took shape exactly on that site. The family, in whose hands it has remained for over six hundred years, still toast "Success to the Hawthorn"! Cawdor was provided with a station by the new railway, but in 1857 it was renamed Kildrummie and a year later disappeared from the timetable for ever, illustrating that bad luck invariably follows a change of name.

Passing beneath the A96, the railway reaches Gollanfield, erstwhile junction for the Fort George branch. Fort George, as with its perhaps more widely known counterparts, Augustus and William, was built precisely to keep the Highlands well and truly under London's thumb, following the Jacobite Rebellion of 1745. Fort Augustus and Fort William developed into centres of commerce, but Fort George, remote on its spit of land jutting out into the Moray Firth, remains an intimidating military establishment, an outstanding example of 18th century military architecture, still in use as a garrison, but also open to the public. The main line station at

Moray Firth

beach *harbour* *National Cycle Route 1*

Nairn

NAIRN

loop

Nairn County FC

R. Nairn

National Cycle Route 1

A96

A939

9

B9092

(*Kildrummie - clsd. 1858*)

Moss-side

Course of Fort George Railway

Gollanfield

(*Gollanfield - clsd. 1965*)

Seafields Restaurant

Lochside

Loch Flemington

Old Military Road

A96

Inverness Airport

Terminal

10

(*Dalcross - clsd. 1965*)

Castle Stuart

11

timber works

A96

Gollanfield was known as Fort George until the branch opened in 1899, whereafter it was known as Gollanfield Junction until 1959. The branch was only 1 mile and 38 chains long, its simple terminus - consisting of a single platform and run-round loop, a goods shed and an engine shed - being located at Ardersier, almost the same distance short of the fort itself! The last passenger trains (public, for the use of) ran in 1943, but troop trains continued to use the line until it was abandoned completely in 1958. An alarming collision occurred at Gollanfield in 1953 between an eastbound passenger and a westbound goods. Three of the four footplatemen involved were killed, and the passenger locomotive, a 1920 built Caledonian Railway 4-4-0, was so badly damaged that it had to be cut up on the spot. It was a Forres based engine, No. 54481.

The origins of Inverness (or Dalcross) Airport lie with the Second World War though there had been suggestions that the site might be developed for passenger air traffic just prior to 1939. In its early years it proved susceptible to flooding. Tarmac runways were put in, and they might well have been the first in Britain. At first the aerodrome had associations with the ill-fated Defiant aircraft and many crashes ensued. One, of a less

serious nature, resulted in the airplane crash-landing on a sandbank in the Moray Firth, from which it was ignominiously rescued by a team of horses. Later in the war the aerodrome was used as a base for missions to Norway, a round trip of over seven hundred miles. Wartime memories were brought back into focus when the airport was used during the making of the 1963 film *633 Squadron*, during which the few surviving serviceable Mosquitos were mustered for action sequences over Glencoe and the Great Glen. There have been proposals that Dalcross station might usefully be re-opened to serve the airport. The timber works to the south of the line just beyond the site of the old station receives timber carried by rail from Kinbrace on the Far North line, though unfortunately, this has to be transhipped into lorries at Inverness for the last few miles of its journey, there no longer being a siding by the works. Castle Stuart was built in 1625 by the Earl of Moray. Over the centuries it has been lived in and left empty in almost equal measure. Latterly it was an hotel which attracted much custom by virtue of its haunted reputation. Now it is a private residence, so perhaps its ghosts are left in peace.

Lattice shadows on Nairn's station footbridge.

From the old kirkyard, an Aberdeen train is seen crossing Nairn Viaduct.

11

Beauly Firth

North Kessock

Kessock Bridge

Moray Firth

The Black Isle

sewage plant

•Standing Stones
(Allanfearn - clsd. 1965)

Balloch

swingbridge

Inverness Caledonian
◇ Thistle FC

A9

Caledonian
Canal

Clachnaharry

Harbour
Branch

Culloden

EWS
Depot

Welsh's Bridge
Junction

Millburn
Junction

Ness Viaduct

A96 retail
park

Cradlehall
Junction

Smithton

Drummossie Muir

(Culloden Moor - clsd. 1965)

INVERNESS

From Dingwall

i 🏛 ⊢ ✕ 🚌

Culloden Battlefield
Visitor Centre

Westhill

River Nairn

Culloden or
Nairn Viaduct

From Perth

LAST laps don't come much more engaging than this line's diminuendo approach along the south bank of Moray Firth towards Inverness. There are standing stones south of the line before Allanfearn, but inevitably, all eyes are drawn towards the glistening firth and an horizon formed by the Black Isle. Across the water lies Munlochy Bay, an obvious indentation, a tidal inlet favoured by greylag geese in the winter. To its left as you look is the remote village of Kilmuir and, adjoining it, Ord Hill, a dominant peak in the context of the view, but only 633ft at its highest point. From this vantage the Black Isle could quite literally be an island, though reference to an atlas will reveal its less romantic status as a peninsular striking out into the sea between Moray and Cromarty firths. Once it had its own railway, a branch from Muir of Ord to Fortrose, whilst the Highland Railway had schemes for a ferry linking Fortrose with Ardersier which never came to fruition.

A sewage plant intervenes to mar the view, but its very necessary function should overide any aesthetic considerations, after all, Inverness's water and sewage arrangements are products of the same era as the railways, before the middle of the 19th century its citizens were using the River Ness simultaneously as a drain and as a source of drinking water! Wading birds and wildfowl gathered on the shoreline create a more pleasant image as you draw ever closer to Inverness. In the distance you'll see the Kessock Bridge opened in 1982 as part of the A9 trunk road improvements, and replacing a vehicular ferry which plied its trade across the narrowest point which separates the Moray and Beauly firths. The stadium you can see, perched on the water's edge, belongs to Inverness Caledonian Thistle Football Club. Nearby, on land now occupied by a trading estate, Inverness's original Municipal Airport was opened by the Duchess of Sutherland in 1933. It owed its existence to the

pioneer aviator Ernest Edmund Fresson, who began flying the mails from Inverness to Kirkwall in the Orkney Islands. A statue of Fresson to be found at the present Inverness Airport marks his achievements. On 17th June 1933, a grand ball was held at the Station Hotel to celebrate the new air service, all of which brings us back to the railway as the Aberdeen line passes beneath the main line from Perth (see *Iron Road to the Highlands*) and your train slows to encounter the pointwork at Millburn Junction. When the line to Nairn was proposed a Mr Welsh of Millburn House objected to the railway for fear that it would 'injure his policies', perhaps, therefore, he doesn't really deserve to be immortalised by the railway at Welsh's Bridge Junction, your reminder that the train is about to draw to a halt at Inbhir Nis's uniquely Y shaped terminus. A floral replica of the Reverend Awdry's tank engine *Percy* greets you on the platform, as do the seagulls overhead. All termini invoke a sense of Journeys' Ending, though here, opportunity knocks to press on north to Kyle of Lochalsh or Wick and Thurso; indeed, one Aberdeen train sheds a portion for The Kyle, which goes through the time-honoured protocol of reversing out of the station to effect its passage north. Resist the temptation to make a bee-line for the city centre. The station purlieus are worthy of attention. Remember that lattice girder bridge spanning the Spey? The plaques from Joseph Mitchell's box girder original are attached to either side of a support column at the end of platforms 5/6, having been placed there when the original bridge was rebuilt in 1906. They form a fittingly emotional end to our journey from Aberdeen, for we have travelled not only through space, but through time as well, encountering a Scotland ostensibly unspoilt by progress, an outlying land where chronology turns out, unexpectedly, to be a witness of the most unreliable kind. All one can do is head for Robbie's Bar in the Royal Highland (nee Station) Hotel and drown one's suspicions and equivocalities with the ghosts of railwaymen and travellers past.

Approach to Inverness
With milepost 140 measuring the distance from Perth via Dava, and with a linespeed of 70mph, the railway runs alongside Moray Firth with the Kessock Bridge in the distance.

GAZETTEER

Aberdeen Harbour as seen from the Maritime Museum

If there's a moral to this guide book at all, it is that you should not sit slavishly on the train, but that you should get off and explore the often achingly beautiful countryside it links you to. We are not Egon Ronay, we are not the Scottish Mountaineering Club, we are not the local Chamber of Commerce, all the facilities and suggestions listed in this gazetteer are by way of being ideas for your own personal development; points of departure if you prefer. To the best of our knowledge the entries are accurate at the time of going to press, but we would urge you to use the telephone or the internet to check ahead of your journey for your own peace of mind. Make good use of the local Tourist Information Centres who are unfailingly courteous and models of patience and humour in the face of the most inane tourist enquiry.

ABERDEEN

Map 1

Remote in its east coast eyrie, it's possible to forget that Scotland's 'third city' is a substantial commercial centre, seaport and holiday resort all wrapped up in one. Ideally, this Granite City needs sunlight to do it justice. Under dull skies it looks, well, *dull*; but when the sun is shining its pink and grey buildings positively glow and are seen at their best. Not an easy city to assimilate, Aberdeen perplexes the first time visitor with a befuddled street layout, arranged, it seems, on several layers, so that you're forever passing under streets or crossing over them. Leaving the station, set your compass

to the north-east, traverse a labyrinth of Wynds and Rows, and ultimately (and entertainingly) sooner or later you'll find yourself emerging on to Union Street, the main thoroughfare whose eastern end is dominated by the Town House and Tolbooth towers, the Mercat Cross and the Salvation Army Citadel. Before exploring further, it may be wise to turn down into Shiprow, location of the Tourist Information Centre. This is perhaps Aberdeen's oldest surviving street. It offers a fine view over the harbour where P&O's ferries berth before setting sail for Orkney and Shetland. Adjoining the TIC is Provost Ross's House and the excellent Maritime Museum

where, if you're not firm with yourself, you might be beguiled into spending your whole stay in Aberdeen!

But it would be a shame (if pardonable) not to delve deeper into this fascinating city, notable for its proliferation of statues. Amongst others, you'll encounter Robert Burns, Gordon of Khartoum, Edward VII, and an especially heroic likeness of William Wallace, so large and bristling that the former Stalinist statues of countries beyond the Iron Curtain are brought to mind. Wallace overlooks the Union Terrace Gardens which parallel the railway as it leaves Aberdeen for the north. This must have been a pleasant location for train watchers in the past with D40s, B1s, and B12s to ogle - nowadays there is not enough variety in rolling stock to make it irresistible. Three great buildings provide a backdrop to the gardens: the Central Library, St Mark's Church and his Majesty's Theatre. Generations of dour Aberdonian wits have nicknamed these Education, Salvation and Damnation respectively.

Accommodation
STATION HOTEL - Guild Street. Tel: 01224 587214. Formerly a railway-owned hotel dating from 1902, now providing comfortable and inexpensive two star accommodation adjacent to the station. THISTLE CALEDONIAN - Union Terrace. Tel: 01224 640233. Four star hotel offering views over Union Terrace Gardens and the railway.

Eating Out
It is necessary to 'nose out' Aberdeen's culinary highlights. Oddly enough they seem themed with certain streets, so that in Correction Wynd you stumble on French cooking at LA CLOCHE (Tel: 01224 644166) and LA BONNE BAGUETTE (Tel: 01224 644445) whilst on Union Terrace the emphasis is Italian as manifested by PAVAROTTI'S (Tel: 01224 622555) and CARMINE'S (Tel: 01224 624145). While we're on Union Terrace you may care to make a mental note of the Thistle Caledonian Hotel's lively CALEY CAFE BAR (Tel: 01224 640233). ARCHIBALD SIMPSON'S (Tel: 01224 621365) on the corner of Union Street and King Street (near the Mercat Cross) is a Wetherspoons conversion of a former bank designed by its namesake, Aberdeen's pre-eminent Victorian architect. Two good restaurants for seafood (both requiring a taxi from the station) are SILVER DARLING (Tel: 01224 576229) by the North Pier and The OLIVE TREE (Tel: 01224 316054) on Queen's Road out on the fashionable western edge of the city.

Shopping
Union Street - 'the Granite Mile' - is Aberdeen's traditional retail thoroughfare and it still hosts some long standing establishments like ESSLEMONT & MACINTOSH, a department store of the old school. Modern retail therapy can be enjoyed (or endured?) in the Bon Accord, St Nicholas and Trinity centres, but off the beaten track you will find smaller, more independent outlets of character and concern for one's more arcane needs in life - try Thistle Street (at the west end of Union Street) to see just how fashionable Aberdeen can be.

Things to Do
TOURIST INFORMATION - Shiprow. Tel: 01224 288828.
ABERDEEN MARITIME MUSEUM - Shiprow. Tel: 01224 337700.

Absolutely first rate interpretation of Aberdeen's rich maritime past and present - fishing, shipping and oil - imaginatively housed in a former church overlooking the harbour itself, so that despite the lack of preserved craft, a real sense of the sea is invoked. Exhibits spill over into Provost Ross's adjoining 16th century house, particularly illustrating the development of whaling, trawling and shipbuilding with some beautiful models of Aberdeen built clippers on display. Shop and cafe.

ABERDEEN ART GALLERY - Schoolhill. Tel: 01224 523700. An astonishing surprise! Aberdeen's art gallery hosts a first rate collection which would rival displays in many cities throughout Europe. Of interest to those of railway bent are Eric Ravilious's *Train Landscape* - a view looking out from an old fashioned 3rd class compartment on to a landscape dominated by a chalk horse - and Robert Brough's *View of Elgin* dated 1894, depicting a train in the foreground travelling towards Aberdeen on the Moray Coast line. Ironically, Brough was to die in a railway accident near Sheffield in 1905. Of particular regional significance is the work of the Aberdonian artist William Dyce, a friend of Prince Albert. Travelling exhibitions, a good shop and a cafe add to the gallery's appeal.

GORDON HIGHLANDERS MUSEUM - Viewfield Road. Tel: 01224 311200. Open April to October but not on Mondays. Moving tribute to the history and tradition of one of the British Army's most celebrated regiments. Gift shop and tea room.

Transport Connections
TAXIS - Don Cabs, Bridge of Don. Tel: 01224 828828.
BUSES - Guild Street bus station lies alongside the railway station and boasts a Travel Shop. Tel: 01224 212266 for Stagecoach services; 01224 650065 for local services.
CAR HIRE - Melville's, Broomhill Road. Book in advance and they'll meet you at the station. Tel: 0870 160 9999.

DUFFTOWN   *Map 6A*
Assuming you have reached Dufftown by rail, it's refreshing to discover that one of this agreeable 'wee toon's' most famous sons is George Stephen, banker, financier and a leading light in the construction of the Canadian Pacific Railway. His exploits are commemorated by the Clock Tower. A cousin, Donald Smith of Forres, also dabbled in the fortunes of TransCanadian railroads. Completed in 1839, the Clock Tower once housed the gaol, now it houses the Tourist Information Centre, which just goes to show how far civilisation has progressed.

Accommodation
FIFE ARMS HOTEL - The Square. Tel: 01340 820220. Small one star hotel.
TANNOCHBRAE - Fife Street. Tel: 01340 820541. Very comfortable guest house plus licensed restaurant.

Eating & Drinking
LA FAISANDERIE - Balvenie Street. Tel: 01340 821273. French restaurant, a pleasant find!
GLENFIDDICH RESTAURANT - Church Street. Tel: 01340 820363. Long established restaurant offering the likes of steaks and fresh

The Clock Tower, Dufftown.

Spey salmon.
A TASTE OF SPEYSIDE - Balvenie Street. Tel: 01340 820860. Restaurant specialising in the fresh cooking of local produce. *Several lively inns, tea rooms and takeaways as well, plus at least two fish & chip shops.*

Shopping
For a relatively small town, Dufftown hosts an interesting array of shops: one could happily spend days ambling (gradually more erratically) between DUFFTOWN BOOKSHOP (secondhand) and THE WHISKY SHOP, a specialist outlet offering at least three hundred single malts and a good choice of Scottish beers to boot. Also of interest is Ann Higgins's Kilt Shop - Tel: 01340 821136.

Things to Do
TOURIST INFORMATION - The Square. Tel: 01340 820501.
KEITH & DUFFTOWN RAILWAY - Tel: 01340 821181. Weekend train rides - Easter to October - on 'The Malt Whisky Line'. See Map 6A.
GLENFIDDICH DISTILLERY - Tel: 01340 820373. Open weekdays all year round plus weekends in the high season. Picturesque distillery founded in 1887 and makers of one of the world's most famous malts. Rare nowadays in that the whisky is bottled on site.
BALVENIE CASTLE - Tel: 01340 820121. Fine 13th century ruined castle overlooking the railway. It belonged to the fearsome Comryn family whose motto was: 'seize your chance and fill your coffers'. Open daily April to September inclusive.

Transport Connections
TAXIS - HOME JAMES, Tel: 01340 821400.
BUSES - Stagecoach service 326 links with Elgin via Craigellachie. Tel: 01343 544222.

DRUMMUIR   *Map 6A*
A remote and bosky halt on the Keith & Dufftown Railway, Drummuir offers delightful opportunities for walkers, the local estate having (with admirable public spirit) waymarked three trails of duration differing between forty minutes and two hours. A less strenuous option is to stroll to Botriphnie kirk or Drummuir Castle's walled garden where seasonal organically grown produce is on sale. Tel: 01542 810225.

DYCE   *Map 1*
Strictly for plane-spotters, Dyce is a conglomerate of industrial concerns centred on the airport.

Eating & Drinking
OSPREY - fish & chips from the old station building.

Things to Do
Follow the Formartine & Buchan Way along the old trackbed of the Buchan line or stay on the train!

Transport Connections
ABERDEEN AIRPORT - Tel: 01224 722331.

ELGIN   *Map 8*
What a handsome 'city' Elgin is, and how it repays exploration! An ancient sense of calm descends as soon as you put the ring road behind you and ascend Moss, Academy or Reidhaven streets towards the centre through quiet backwaters of handsome villas. Breasting a rise, streets of small shops lead down to a spacious High Street loomed over by St Giles, an outstanding church of the early 19th century, designed in Greek Revival style by Aberdeen's celebrated architect, Archibald Simpson. This wonderful building, in its spacious setting, sets the tone for the rest of this neo-classical town, or more exactly, 'city'. City, because Elgin is graced by a cathedral, albeit a cathedral in ruins since the Reformation, though substantial in decay and enhanced by its proximity to a Biblical Garden planted with every species of plant named in the Bible. Other significant buildings and structures include the domed Gray's Hospital at the west end of High Street, the Duke

of Gordon's column (soaring 80ft high above the old Castle Hill) and the reconstructed Muckle Cross which stands beside St Giles. An entertaining and informative Town Trail leaflet is available free of charge from the Tourist Information Centre at the eastern end of the High Street. Equipped with this, visitors can perambulate Elgin at their own pace and with their own interests uppermost in mind. That inveterate traveller and chronicler, Daniel Defoe, got it just about right when he summed Elgin up as 'a very agreeable place to live in'!

Accommodation
LAICHMORAY HOTEL - Maisondieu Road. Tel: 01343 540045. Three star hotel formerly known as the Station Hotel.

Eating & Drinking
ABBEY COURT RESTAURANT - Greyfriars Street. Tel: 01343 542849. Italian/Scots cooking in comfortable atmosphere within easy walking distance of the station.
FAILTE - Batchen Street. Homely little cafe for hungry travellers. Tel: 01343 546361.
TAPAS DEL MUNDO - Shepherd's Close. Tel: 01343 549737. The Med meets Morayshire!
THUNDERTON HOUSE - High Street. Breakfasts, lunches and teas in a 16th century building where Bonnie Prince Charlie reputedly slept before Culloden. Tel: 01343 554921.
IONIC BAR - High Street. Dark little drinking den - atmospheric, but not for the faint-hearted! Tel: 01343 542118.

Shopping
Eschew the siren call of the stationside ASDA and explore, instead, the little streets of the town. Here you'll come upon characterful independent outlets where service comes with a smile and guid *craic*. Examples: GORDON & MACPHAIL on South Street (Tel: 01343 545111), 'the world's leading malt whisky specialist' established here in 1895 which also features an excellent deli counter; J.C.Dawson on Batchen Street (Tel: 01343 542243) butcher and purveyor of prize-winning steak pies; YEADON'S BOOKSHOP on Greyfriar's Street (Tel: 01343 542411) and SONYA in the High Street (Tel: 01343 549111) a designer clothing outlet of some style and panache.

Things to Do
TOURIST INFORMATION - High Street. Tel: 01343 542666.
ELGIN MUSEUM - High Street. Tel: 01343 543675. Open daily April to October. Very interesting and enjoyable displays and interpretations of local history.
GLEN MORAY DISTILLERY - Bruceland Road. Tel: 01343 542577. Located on the western edge of Elgin and originally a brewery, visits to this distillery are delightfully informal, so much so that you will probably be shown around by a true distillery worker as opposed to a tour guide.
SPYNIE PALACE - National Trust for Scotland. Former residence of the Bishops of Moray. Open April to September. Tel: 01343 546358.
MORAY MOTOR MUSEUM - Bridge Street. Tel: 01343 544933. Open daily Easter to October 11am-5pm. Fascinating collection of cars, motorcycles and automobilia housed in former mill.

Sueno's Stone - Forres

PLUSCARDEN ABBEY - Tel: 01343 890257. 8 miles south-west of Elgin, rail travellers are best taking a taxi. Open daily from 4.45am! Though dating back to the 13th century, the monks left at the time of the Reformation, only returning in 1948. Well worth a visit if time permits. Retreats available for those in need of a battery recharge.
BAXTERS HIGHLAND VILLAGE - Fochabers, 9 miles east of Elgin. Bus connections - service 305. Tel: 01343 820666. Entertaining centre celebrating the history of this increasingly famous soup maker: shops, restaurants, culinary demonstrations and museum. Ask them politely why they don't re-open the railway to Orbliston Junction!

Transport Connections
CAR HIRE - Alan Milne, Station Road. Tel: 01343 542254.
BUSES - useful non-rail connections to Dufftown (service 326), the Moray Coast (service 305), Findhorn and Kinloss (services 310-318). Tel: 01343 544222.

TAXIS - City Taxis: Tel: 01343 543555. Moray Taxis: Tel: 01343 542665.
CYCLE HIRE - Bikes & Bowls, High Street. Tel: 01343 549656.

FORRES
Map 9
Architecturally well-endowed, Forres betrays an unnecessary lack of self-confidence in the art of wooing visitors. Perhaps it's just shy, perhaps its citizens prefer their own company. Whatever the source of its reticence, it should not dissuade the discerning visitor from alighting at the station and proceeding (by way of Bridge Street) to the town centre, an imposing thoroughfare dominated by the William Robertson's elaborate cupola-topped Tolbooth of 1838. En route they'll encounter an obelisk of Peterhead granite perched on the old castle hill, former court of King Duncan. That isn't what the monument commemorates, rather it is dedicated to the memory of a surgeon who dies from exhaustion in the Crimea. He hailed from Cromarty, but the citizens of that town were apathetic in erecting a monument, so a friend caused it to be built in Forres. A nice story suggests that on certain days of brilliant sunshine, the light bounces off the obelisk and shines in the eyes of the unwitting folk of Cromarty, fifteen miles across the Moray Firth. Also on the way in stands St Laurence's Church, an ebullient Edwardian building dating from 1904 and the town's commercial heyday as a railway junction. To continue beyond the Tolbooth is equally rewarding. Equally, the more inquisitive visitor might be beguiled by the town's alleys and wynds. One would lack ambition, however, were one not to climb Cluny Hill and ascend the Nelson Tower , or proceed to the eastern edge of the town and pay homage to Sueno's Stone, a twenty-three foot high monument dating from possibly as long ago as the 9th century, but looking a tad incongruous now in its well-meant glass box.

Accommodation
KNOCKOMIE HOTEL - Grantown Road. Tel: 01309 673146. Four star country house hotel.
RAMNEE HOTEL - Victoria Road. Tel: 01309 672410. Four star hotel near Sueno's Stone.

Eating & Drinking
ROSSINI'S - High Street. Tel: 01309 676500. Pasta/pizza, restaurant/take-away.
SCOTCH OVEN TEAROOM - Ashers Bakery, High Street. Tel: 01309 672635.

Shopping
A new TESCO was opening adjacent to the station as we went to press. Up in the town the shopping is useful if uninspired, suggestive of a commercial hinterland not easily impressed by twenty-first century consumerism.

Things to Do
TOURIST INFORMATION - High Street. Tel: 01309 672938.
THE FALCONER MUSEUM - Tolbooth Street. Tel: 01309 673701. A charming little museum devoted to Forres's past and its personalities from Lord Strathcona the locally born railway magnate to Roy Williamson of The Corries folk duo who spent the last eight

years of his life in the town.

NELSON TOWER - open when the flag flies from its battlemented top, ninety-six steps up. Great vistas of Findhorn Bay.

BENROMACH DISTILLERY - Invererne Road. Tel: 01309 675968. Lineside distillery easily reached from Forres station. Re-opened in its centenary year by Gordon & McPhail after a period of disuse.

FINDHORN HERITAGE CENTRE - Findhorn, 5 miles north of Forres. Tel: 01309 690349. Small museum housed in former salmon fishery huts devoted to the village's local history.

FINDHORN FOUNDATION - Findhorn, bus connections. Tel: 01309 690311. Celebrated centre established in 1962 to forge new attitudes to education, community and the environment. Courses on personal and spiritual growth. Eco-village demonstrates themes for a sustainable future. Visitor centre, gardens, shop and cafe.

BRODIE CASTLE - Brodie, 4 miles west of Forres. Stagecoach Express service No.10 provides hourly links from Elgin bus station and Forres High Street. National Trust for Scotland Z-plan tower house open April to end of September. Tel: 01309 641371.

BRODIE COUNTRYFARE - Brodie, 4 miles west of Forres. Bus links as above. Retail centre for food, clothing, gifts etc. Open daily. Tel: 01309 641555.

Transport Connections

BUSES - Stagecoach connections to/from Brodie (for the castle and the Countryfare centre), Kinloss and Findhorn (for the Findhorn Foundation and coastal walks). Tel: 01343 544222.

TAXIS - Denny's, High Street. Tel: 01309 672180.

CYCLE HIRE - Recycles: Tel: 01309 672811.

HUNTLY

Map 4

Huntly, apparently, was something of a hotbed of missionary zeal, intent on sending its sons to the dark continent and beyond to do good works. An impressive number of its inhabitants also went out into the wider world and made fortunes for themselves. One wonders how any of them could bear to leave, for this is an adorable 'wee toon' cupped in a bowl of hills and laid out largely on an 18th century gridiron plan, its two main streets intersecting in a spacious square overlooked by handsome public buildings and hotels. Cynosure of the square is a statue commemorating the 5th Duke of Richmond who succeeded the last Duke of Gordon. Accompanying it are the 'Stannin Steens o' Strathbogie, two Pictish symbol stones which once formed part of a stone circle. Two marble seats bear quotations from the works of George MacDonald. Of perhaps greater interest to railway enthusiasts is the survival of a Scottish Region pale blue enamel sign at the corner of Duke Street pointing to the station!

There are too many significant buildings in Huntly to provide an inventory here. Confining ourselves to highlights, therefore, we would draw your attention to the robust Town Hall with its imposing clock tower, Alexander Scott's 'eventide home' on Gladstone Road, the Catholic St Margaret's Chapel, and the Clydesdale Bank which is the work of the feted Aberdeen architect Archibald Simpson. To the north of the town lies Huntly Castle, best approached through the arched gateway to the old Gordon Schools - again the work of

Huntly Castle

Archibald Simpson. En route you'll pass the elegant pavilion of Huntly Cricket Club. Another sporting activity flourished nearby in the shape of Huntly's Nordic Ski Centre, a cross-country skiing course on artificial track. The castle itself, perched above the river Deveron, comes as no anti-climax, its 16th century remains providing a dramatic end to a memorable walk.

Accommodation

THE GORDON ARMS HOTEL - The Square. Tel: 01466 792288. Modest, yet comfortable two star hotel in the centre of town, 5 minutes walk from the station.

HUNTLY HOTEL - The Square. Tel: 01466 792703. Small two star hotel, as above.

CASTLE HOTEL - Tel: 01466 792696. Impressive 18th century country house hotel, once the home of the Dukes of Gordon. Three stars.

Eating & Drinking

Bar meals at the hotels are your best bet. Alternatively there are Chinese and Indian takeaways plus an excellent fish & chip shop (Tel: 01466 792278) on Bogie Street less than 5 minutes walk from the station. Teas, coffees and light meals are available from the MERRY KETTLE on Duke Street - Tel: 01466 792108.

Shopping

Imagine you're in some back of beyond town in the west of Ireland and you'll have Huntly in focus - and that is intended as a compliment! Friendly little shops cater for most needs, though a SOMERFIELD supermarket does lurk in the backstreets if you feel disenfranchised from 21st century reality without one. SCOTT the butcher on Duke Street was Scotland's 2001 'Haggis Champion'; FORBES & RAEBURN on Bogie Street vies for your custom, as does GORDON RHIND on Gordon Street. Nearby, RIZZA'S are purveyors of extremely tasty home made ice cream in the Italian tradition. There are two or three good bakers as well, together with a small branch of W.H.SMITH. Banks, chemists, hardwear, and clothing shops complete the picture, along with a small secondhand bookshop on Deveron Road. On the south-western edge of town you'll find DEAN'S shortbread factory shop which deals in local crafts and gifts as well - Tel: 01466 792086.

Things to Do
TOURIST INFORMATION - The Square. Tel: 01466 792255.
HUNTLY CASTLE - Tel: 01466 793191. Beautiful ruin in a beautiful setting. Open daily throughout the summer, winter openings daily ex Thur pm & Fri.

Transport Connections
CAR HIRE - G & L MARSHALL - Millyard (adjacent railway station) Tel: 01466 792594.
TAXIS - Deveron Taxis, Tel: 01466 794949.
BUSES - Tel: 01224 212266. Stagecoach Express Service 10 runs to Inverurie via Pitcaple.

INSCH
Map 3

Surrounded by great rolling farmlands studded with antiquities, the West Garioch (pronounced 'geary') village of Insch is the walker's railhead for Bennachie and is also a centre for a number of waymarked cycle routes on local roads. One of these, the 'Lenchie Loop', takes in the Picardy Stone, a particularly fine example of a Pictish symbol stone. Nearer at hand, one may make the fairly steep ascent to the top of Dunnideer, or go forest walking on the slopes of the Hill of Christ's Kirk. And if all the foregoing sounds too energetic, why not simply sit on a station bench, soak up the countryside and listen out for the occasional rustle of the signal wires.

Accommodation
CARRIAGES - Commercial Road (opposite the station) - Tel: 01464 820604. Well-appointed pub accommodation and bar food. Formerly known as the Station Hotel.
COMMERCIAL HOTEL - Commerce Street. Tel: 01464 820209. Small hotel - high teas available.

Eating & Drinking
FAST FRYS - Western Road. Tel: 01464 820500. Fish & chip restaurant & take away.

Shopping
McCREATH's - Muriel Jonassen's kiltmaking concern - is housed in the station. Tel: 01464 821313. If you can drag yourself away, you'll find the centre of Insch about five minutes walk to the north. It's refreshing to encounter a village where the butcher and baker, twin bedrocks of rural retailing, still flourish independently. Respectively they are: FINDLAY & LEIPER on High Street and JACK COOPER ('The Baker Fae The Back O' Bennachie') on Commerce Street. Other bastions of commerce include the unusual combination of a chemist and stationer, a Costcutter general store (within a rather nicely framed facade) and branches of the Clydesdale and Lloyds TSB banks. Not a shop as such, but worthy of the note of railway enthusiasts, is THE TRANSPORT

TREASURY, Barry Hoper's extensive photographic archive of transport images. Tel: 01464 820863.

Things to Do
THE INSCH CONNECTION - Railway Station. Tel: 01464 821354. Open April to September, Wednesday and Saturday afternoons. Charming collection of rail and local history artefacts enhanced by a splendid model of Insch station in its heyday. Look out for the model of the GNoS 4-4-0 locomotive named *Benachie* - and yes, the GNoS only used one 'N'!
ARCHAEOLINK PREHISTORY PARK - Oyne, 3 miles east of Insch. Tel: 01464 851500. If only there was still a railway station at Oyne, this increasingly popular visitor attraction would benefit from an influx of tourists arriving by environmentally sustainable transport, your alternative is to book a taxi from Insch, or, even better, take your bike onto the train and cycle to Oyne from Insch. Perhaps in more enlightened times to come the station will be resurrected specifically to serve this award-winning centre's celebration of prehistoric Scotland, featuring Stone Age, Iron Age and Roman period interpretations of the distant past which will

Station Square, Inverness

appeal to all age groups. Open daily April to October. Shop and cafe.

Transport Connections
TAXIS - Insch Country Cabs, Tel: 01464 821365.

INVERNESS
Map 11

It must be hoped that Inverness's recently acquired city status doesn't go to the Highland capital's head. Already perfectly formed, there is scant need for spurious defining accolades, let alone unnecessary growth, the burgeoning Eastgate Centre is in danger of out-scaling the station, let alone the surrounding streets. Walk straight out of the station and the centre embraces you without formality. Saunter through the close-packed streets (which all, eventually, appear to lead to the riverbank) and you're likely to feel immediately at home. Not a lot of people know that Inverness is the only place outside of London where the Cabinet has met. We'll leave it to your curiosity to discover under what circumstances!

Accommodation
ROYAL HIGHLAND HOTEL - Station Square. Tel: 01463 231926. Former Station Hotel dating back to Highland Railway days and still redolent of that golden era though no longer do 'porters meet every train'! Three stars and not the most economical hotel in town but worth staying in for its grandiloquent atmosphere and proximity to the station.
GLEN MHOR HOTEL - Ness Bank. Comfortable three star hotel in riverside setting with good restaurants. Tel: 01463 234308.
TRAVEL INN - Millburn Road. Lodge style accommodation in hotel 10 minutes walk from railway station. Tel: 01463 712010.
YOUTH HOSTEL - Victoria Drive. 7 minutes walk from station off Millburn Road. Tel: 01463 231771.

Eating Out
THE MUSTARD SEED - corner of Bank and Fraser streets. Open 12-3pm and 6-10pm daily. Lively and modern riverside restaurant which would not seem out of place in Edinburgh or Glasgow. Highly personable young staff serve memorable meals at surprisingly inexpensive prices. Tel: 01463 220220.
QISMAT TANDOORI - Millburn Road. Tel: 01463 716020. Indian restaurant near station.
THE AULD DISTILLERY - Millburn Road - informal 'Beefeater' restaurant adjunct to Travel Inn, overlooking railway sidings, ten minutes walk from station. Tel: 01463 712010.
PALIO - Queensgate. Tel: 01463 711950. Pasta and pizza in pleasant surroundings.
LEAKEY'S - Church Street. Homely cafe serving soups, open sandwiches and salads etc within secondhand bookshop premises. Daily soup, inexpensive, flavoursome and nourishing. Tel: 01463 239947.

Shopping
The compact city centre means that nearly everything's within rushing back for your train distance of the station. High Street and Bridge Street are the main thoroughfares - the former being pedestrianised. Elsewhere, highlights are the VICTORIAN MARKET

tucked away between the shop fronts on Academy Street, Union Street and Queensgate and readily visible from the Station Square. Its uncannily railway like architecture dates from 1891, the result of extensive rebuilding after a fire. Also on Union Street you might look out for THE GOURMET'S LAIR, a discrete little delicatessen offering some nice lines in local food and drink. Bookworms should make a bee line for LEAKEY'S on Church Street, reputedly Scotland's largest secondhand and antiquarian bookseller where there's usually quite a good selection of rail related titles. Tel: 01463 239947. More practically, there's a large SAFEWAY branch on Millburn Road just 3 minutes walk from the station.

Things to Do
TOURIST INFORMATION CENTRE - Castle Wynd. Tel: 01463 234353.
WALKING TOURS - guided tours of the city centre from the Tourist Information Centre on Castle Wynd. Tel: 07730 831069.
GUIDE FRIDAY - open top bus tours of Inverness, Culloden and Loch Ness. An excellent way to get a 'feel' for the vicinity. Tel: 01463 224000.
JACOBITE CRUISES - cruises on the Caledonian Canal throughout the summer from Tomnahurich Bridge, approx 1 mile from city centre. Tel: 01463 233999.
MORAY FIRTH CRUISES - short sea cruises from Inverness Harbour. Tel: 01463 717900.
MUSEUM & ART GALLERY - Castle Wynd. Local and highland heritage centre. Tel: 01463 237114.
CULLODEN MOOR VISITOR CENTRE - Culloden Moor. Approx 5 miles east of city centre; access for rail travellers by No. 12 bus or taxi. Tel: 01463 790607.
A 'Day Trips from Inverness' leaflet is produced annually describing numerous travel opportunities by train, bus and ferry to make the most of a stay in the locality. Contact the TIC on 01463 234353 or the ScotRail Travel Centre on 01463 239026 for further details.

Transport Connections
BUSES - Bus station adjacent to railway station. For all local transport information telephone the Highland Council helpline on 01463 702458.
CAR HIRE - Sharps Reliable Wrecks - Tel: 01463 236684. Office handily located on station concourse. Thrifty Car Rental, Harbour Road: 7 mins walk from station but if you pre-book they'll meet you off the train. Tel: 01463 224466. Melville's Self Drive, Harbour road. Tel: 01463 221669.
TAXIS - Rank Radio Taxis - 111 Academy Street. Tel: 01463 221111.
CYCLE HIRE - Barneys - 35 Castle Street. Tel: 01463 232249. Open throughout the year 9am-9pm.

INVERURIE
Map 2

A proud wee burgh with a rich history and a handsome Town Hall, Inverurie lies at the meeting of the rivers Don and Urie or Ury. Adjacent to this confluence stand the Bass and Little Bass, a motte and bailey stronghold dating from the 12th century. Indeed, the strategic significance of the rivers led to many battles being fought

The Harlaw Monument, Bennachie in the background.

in the vicinity through the ages, the last being at the time of the 1745 Jacobite Rebellion. Inverurie's most famous son is the poet and musician William Thom, a somewhat tragic figure who died penniless at the age of 49. Thom was born in Aberdeen in 1798 and was a weaver, a precarious trade to be employed in at the best of times. Poetry briefly offered a financial lifeline, and on the publication of his best known poem *The Mitherless Bairn* he gained the backing of a number of wealthy admirers and was briefly feted by literary society, not least Charles Dickens and Thomas Carlyle. Sadly, fame went to his head and a profligate lifestyle soon lost him the money his poetry had made. In debt, he left Inverurie in a 'moonlit flit' and

soon after died in Dundee. His common law wife Jean (who died of typhus fever at the age of 27, outlasting Thom by just a few weeks) is buried in an unmarked grave in the cemetery by The Bass.

Accommodation
KINTORE ARMS HOTEL - High Street. Tel: 01467 621367. Cosy two star hotel.

Eating & Drinking
TOWNHOUSE RESTAURANT - Market Place. Tel: 01467 621378.

Shopping
Good selection of all facilities within easy walking distance of the station.

Things to Do
TOURIST INFORMATION - High Street. Tel: 01467 625800.
CARNEGIE LIBRARY & MUSEUM - Market Place. Small local history museum open afternoons only.

Transport Connections
BUSES - Tel: 01224 212266.
TAXIS - Kenny's Taxis - Tel: 01467 620609/621486.

KEITH
Maps 6/6A

Self-styled ' the friendly town', Keith doesn't appear to go out of its way to embrace tourism, but one senses that it must be a nice enough place to live in. It was built in three distinct parts. Old Keith is centred on the banks of the Isla, an important source of cleansing and power for the now defunct woollen mills. Along Station Road you'll come upon Milton Tower, all that remains of an ancient castle, seat of the Ogilvie family, of which one John Ogilvie was martyred at Glasgow Cross in 1615 for his strong Catholic beliefs. Make it your business to seek out the Auld Brig which dates from 1609 and which is overlooked by the old kirkyard with its collection of imposing tombs. Nearby is Gaun's Pool, where the friendly folk of Keith habitually drowned witches up until the 18th century. The architecturally imposing New Town was laid out by the Earl of Seafield in the 18th century in a deliberate attempt to ease congestion on the main road between Aberdeen and Inverness. It is formed by a grid of streets centred on the spacious Reidhaven Square. A further development, Fife Keith, lies to the west of the river.

Accommodation
UGIE HOUSE HOTEL - Church Road. Tel: 01542 887671.

Eating & Drinking
BOOGIE WOOGIE - Regent Square (at top end of Station Road, 7 mins walk from station - or 4 mins walk uphill to west of K&D's Town station) Tel: 01542 888077. Characterful gift and coffee shop also serving delicious light meals, a few minutes walk uphill to the west from Keith Town station: local tourist information available.

Shopping
The town's commercial thoroughfare is Mid Street, dominated by a clock towered institute. Unfortunately, many local shops seem to be shutting down, and too many window-fronts are bereft of displays. One particularly handsome ironmonger's frontage has closed its doors for the last time, though another, by name of JAMES ANNAND, happily stands its ground.

Things to Do

KEITH & DUFFTOWN RAILWAY - Tel: 01340 821181. Preserved railway offering scenic rides each weekend to the whisky capital of Dufftown. See Map 6A.

SCOTTISH TARTANS MUSEUM - Mid Street. Tel: 01542 888419. In a town blessed with a kilt school, it is thoroughly appropriate to find a tartan museum relocated from Edinburgh. One of their most treasured exhibits is a woman's plaid dating from 1726. Of equal interest is John Brown's (Queen Victoria's much trusted servant) Highland suit and underpants! Open Mon-Sat 11am-3pm (4pm Jul & Aug).

SRATHISLA DISTILLERY - Seafield Avenue. Tel: 01542 783044. Founded in 1786, Strathisla is said to be Scotland's oldest operational Highland distillery . Its picturesque pair of pagodas stand just a few hundred yards from the railway station on Seafield Avenue, the main route for rail travellers into the town centre. Self-guided tours are available, plus refreshments and the opportunity to taste a complimentary dram. Furthermore a voucher is redeemable in the distillery shop against the purchase of a bottle of Strathisla Single Malt.

Transport Connections

BUSES - Stagecoach Express Service 10 links with Elgin via Fochabers (for Baxters) and Lhanbryde. Service 309 meets most trains and will take you into town, though the exercise would do you better. 309 also runs to Buckie. Tel: 01343 544222.
TAXIS - F.S.McLean, Station Road - Tel: 01542 882899.

NAIRN
Map 10

Nairn's 'feel-good factor' establishes itself as soon as you walk down the station approach road. It might still be the Nineteen-Fifties and you might be striding purposefully towards the beach with your spade, bucket and windbreak together with a large towel for facilitating the change into your swimming togs with due decorum. Nairn wasn't always so leisure minded. Thomas Telford made some improvements to the harbour here in 1820 and in the mid 19th century the town played host to over a hundred fishing vessels, mainly engaged in the herring trade. Prior to the advent of the railway the harbour was busy with other commodities also. On 3rd November 1853 a schooner docked with 1,200 barrels of coal from the Tyne, returning with a cargo of locally grown potatoes. Nowadays Nairn Harbour provides secure berths for yachts and new housing clusters round the attractive quayside. On either side of the River Nairn's entry into the Moray Firth long stretches of fine white sanded beach lure day-trippers and holidaymakers. In 1943 the Third British Infantry Division used these self-same sands to practise for D-Day. If this was the last they saw of their home country they couldn't have done much better ...

Accommodation

THE WINDSOR HOTEL - Albert Street. Tel: 01667 453108. Three star hotel in the town centre.
SUNNY BRAE HOTEL - Marine Avenue. Tel: 01667 452309. Award-winning small hotel open March-November offering sea views.

Eating & Drinking

THE LONGHOUSE - Harbour Street. Tel: 01667 455532. Nice decor suggests good food at this family-run restaurant.
NAIRN TANDOORI - High Street. Tel: 01667 456293.

Shopping

One main thoroughfare, a side street and a Safeway supermarket sums up Nairn's shopping facilities, but in common with most Scots towns the butchers are excellent, notably BROWNS on High Street and ROBERTSONS on Leopold Street. ASHERS BAKERY has two branches, one at either end of the town - it would be careless of you to leave Nairn without sampling their baked bean and potato pies.

Things to Do

TOURIST INFORMATION - Academy Street. Tel: 01667 452753.
PICCOLO PRINTING MUSEUM - Harbour Street. Tel: 01667 454508. Charming little adjunct to printworks specialising in quality stationery. Highlights include an Albion printing press dating from 1847 and an Arab Platen of 1890.
NAIRN MUSEUM - Viewfield Drive. Tel: 01667 456791. Open Easter to October daily (ex Suns) 10am-4.30pm. If only every small town boasted a museum of local life and lore as conscientious as this.

It occupies a handsome 19th century house approached through an avenue of trees and fronted by a splendid statue to Dr John Grigor, something of a celebrity in these parts. Inside you'll encounter a series of rooms themed to particular aspects of Nairn history. Presentation is hardly 'high tech', but thorough and fascinating. Of Nairn's railway history, for example, you might discover through contemporary extracts from the local newspaper that on 20th September 1855 a considerable crowd awaited the appearance of the first iron horse to reach the town, or that, a few weeks later, with the line completed, the contractors - Brassey & Falshaw - put up for auction twenty-seven 'superior' horses surplus to requirements. Of such magic is local history made.
MORAY FIRTH BOAT TRIPS - Tel: 01667 456078. Trips from Nairn Harbour to see the seals (and possibly also dolphins!) at Ardersier.
FORT GEORGE - Fort George, 6 miles west of Nairn. Tel: 01667 462777.

Transport Connections

BUSES - Stagecoach Express service 10 links with Forres via Brodie. Tel: 01463 239292.
TAXIS - Cawdor Taxis, Tel: 01667 404315.

The sea front, Nairn.